KATE O'BRIEN: A LITERARY PORTRAIT

IRISH LITERARY STUDIES

KATE O'BRIEN:
A LITERARY PORTRAIT

LORNA REYNOLDS

/l

COLIN SMYTHE
Gerrards Cross, Bucks.

BARNES AND NOBLE BOOKS
Totowa, New Jersey
1987

Copyright © 1987 by Lorna Reynolds

First published in 1987 by Colin Smythe Limited
Gerrards Cross, Buckinghamshire

British Library Cataloguing in Publication Data

Reynolds, Lorna
    Kate O'Brien: a literary portrait.
    1. O'Brien, Kate—Criticism and
    interpretation
    I. Title
    823'912   PR6029.B65Z/
    ISBN 0-86140-239-1

First published in 1987 in the United States of America
by Barnes and Noble Books, Totowa, New Jersey 07512

Library of Congress Cataloging in Publication Data

Reynolds, Lorna
    Kate O'Brien: a literary portrait.

    Includes index.
    1. O'Brien, Kate, 1897–1974—Criticism and
    interpretation. I. Title.
    PR6065.B74Z86   1987   823'.912   85-30612
    ISBN 0-389-20613-X

Produced in Great Britain
Set by Crypticks, Leeds,
and printed and bound by Billing & Sons Ltd.
Worcester

'I am influenced by the singing voice and by dance music. Masefield said, "Don't despise dance music; it is the music hearts break to." '

Kate O'Brien in a television programme on Radio Telefís Éireann, originally transmitted in 1974, repeated 6 February 1983.

CONTENTS

PART 1

PART 2

ILLUSTRATIONS

ACKNOWLEDGMENTS

I wish to thank Miss Mary O'Neill, Kate O'Brien's literary executrix, for invaluable help in the writing of this book — the loan of MSS. and documents and for information which she alone possesses; Mrs. Mary O'Mara of Limerick for access to O'Brien family papers, a present of photographs, and most generous hospitality; John and Donogh O'Brien, Kate O'Brien's nephews, for family information and documents.

I also owe a debt of gratitude to my sister, Mrs. Mabel FitzGerald-Smith, for help in research on the Thornhill family; to my niece, Claudia FitzGerald-Smith, for research on the horse-breeding business in Ireland; to my niece, Jennifer Reynolds, for help with the typing, and my niece, Judith Reynolds, for the cover photograph of Limerick.

PART 1

I

ORIGINS AND EARLY LIFE

Certain episodes and dates in Irish History are planted deep in the memory of every Irish child: the defeat of the Danes by King Brian Boru at Clontarf in 1014; the invasion of the Normans on the invitation of Dermot MacMurrough, King of Leinster, in 1169; the march of the Earls from the North, their defeat at the battle of Kinsale in 1603 and flight to the continent; the battle of the Boyne and defeat of King James II; the subsequent siege of Limerick in 1691, the Treaty of Limerick and the departure of the defeated officers and men of the Irish army, the Wild Geese, to serve in the armies of Europe. If a particular child happens to be a native of one or other such celebrated places, then local pride or grief makes the memory ineradicable. Limerick children have a lasting memorial of the Treaty of Limerick — no sooner signed than broken, as the legend goes — in the Treaty Stone. One Limerick child tells how her father, James O'Mara, brought his London-born children to see the Treaty Stone, because his father had brought him when he was a little boy:- 'Every patriotic man in Limerick made a point of telling his children about the broken treaty.'

Though Kate O'Brien hated all manifestations of wars and sieges, all signs of defensiveness in human artifacts, indeed in human beings, she was obliged in her travel book on Ireland, *My Ireland (1962)*, at least to mention the Treaty Stone. She does so disparagingly:-

This undressed lump of limestone sits on a squat, small pedestal: when I was a child I thought it partook in some degree of the sacred, but I did not find it endearing: no one could indeed. [1]

She sees it, however, as more than an ugly record of national defeat, as a symbol of European import, as marking the end, for all practical purposes, of the Jacobite cause, and providing to the terrible

multiplying battle-fields of Europe the gift of the Irish Brigade. The
Irish Brigade was composed of the Wild Geese mentioned above.
They swept through these battlefields with the avenging cry of,
'Remember Limerick!':-

> . . . We were at Ramillies
> We left our bones in Fontenoy,
> And up in the Pyrenees,
> Before Dunkirk, on Landen's Plain,
> Cremona, Lille and Ghent:
> We're all over Austria, France and Spain,
> Wherever they pitched a tent.

It would have meant something to Kate O'Brien, hater of war
though she was, that in the Irish Brigade, Viscount Clare's Regiment
— Clare's Dragoons — figured prominently. Viscount Clare was an
O'Brien, one of Brian Boru's many descendants. It certainly meant
something to her that the Norman Cathedral of Limerick, St.
Mary's, had been built by Donal O'Brien, Prince of Thomond. She
mentions the names of other families whose remains lie beneath the
Cathedral stones — Roches, Perrys, Arthurs, Russells, Sextons —
as 'upstarts' of the eighteenth century, who built the modern city in
its Georgian order. It struck her as distinctly appropriate that a letter
should be delivered to her in Bunratty Castle, when she attended
the reception to celebrate the restoration of the Castle, an O'Brien
stronghold, abandoned since the seventeenth century: for the first
time since the seventeenth century a letter to an O'Brien was
addressed to the castle: and she was the recipient. Without doubt,
pride of blood was part of her nature. I remember once when she
and I had a quarrel and the argument had gone in my favour, she
said suddenly:- 'But how could I hope to get the better of you, with
your rowdy Tipperary ancestors?' To which I replied:- 'If the truth
were known, I dare say there wouldn't be a pin's worth of difference
between *my* rowdy Tipperary ancestors and *your* rowdy Limerick
ones.' The O'Brien name had meant something to her grandfather
when he had had the O'Brien arms emblazoned on the roof-ridge
of the house he had built and called 'Boru House'. The O'Brien
name had meant something to her father when he bought some
historic O'Brien diamonds from the house of the Viscounts Clare
and had them set in an engagement ring for his fiancée, Katty
Thornhill, Kate O'Brien's mother-to-be.

The O'Briens, a prolific and tenacious race, were, like the O'Connors, the O'Neills and the MacCarthys, sovereign princes for many years before the arrival of the Normans in Ireland. They trace their ancestry back to Brian Boru, and he traced his back to Heber, eldest son of Milesius, who is said to have conquered Ireland about 1500 B.C. The branches of the family that are found with English titles of ennoblement take their origin from Turlough, who died in 1528. His eldest son, Conor, ruled as King of Thomond until 1540 when he was succeeded by his youngest brother, Murrough, the Tanist, or Heir-Apparent; Conor's son, Donough, being a minor, could not succeed. Murrough was one of those Irish chieftains who were inveigled into making a formal submission to Henry VIII, by yielding up their Irish titles and the tenure of their lands according to Irish law and accepting in their stead an English title of nobility and a grant of their lands held under English law. The Head of the O'Briens ceded his title of King of Thomond to become Earl of Thomond and Baron Inchiquin. We can only guess at the anxieties, fears, or faint-heartedness that made him do this. On the face of it, it does not seem much of a bargain, and we are told that other members of the family strongly disapproved. From him descends the Inchiquin branch of the O'Briens. By the terms of the creation his nephew, Conor's son Donough succeeded to the Earldom of Thomond, and from him descended the Thomond branch of the family, and the Viscounts Clare, who had remained Catholic and left Ireland for France after the Treaty of Limerick. This elder line from Donough ended in England with the death of the eighth Earl because of an attainder on the heir who was known in France as the sixth Viscount Clare and Maréchal Comte de Thomond. Both titles became extinct with the death of the seventh Viscount in 1774.

From Murrough descended the second line of the O'Briens who became Barons of Inchiquin and lived in Dromoland Castle, now a splendid hotel. There were several other branches of the family, such as the O'Briens of Ara, the Carrigogunell O'Briens, the Aran Island O'Briens, the Waterford O'Briens, the Ballynalacken O'Briens; and their seats were to be found in the counties of Limerick, Clare, Cork, Galway, Waterford and Tipperary. There was a Dutch branch, a Canadian branch, as well as the French branch of the Viscounts Clare. They distinguished themselves in many walks of life, at home and abroad, in the army and the navy, as governors of various English possessions overseas. The Dromoland branch became connected with the royal family of England by the marriage of Sir Lucius O'Brien to Catherine Keightly, first cousin of Queen Mary and Queen Anne, whose mother was Catherine Keightly's aunt.

But the O'Brien name was not limited to the ennobled and distinguished members of the clan. As Kate O'Brien says in *My Ireland* the name O'Brien is not only to be found on the tombstones in St. Mary's Cathedral, but everywhere, in the churchyards, houses, pubs and cottages of Limerick and Clare. These humbler representatives had, of course, remained Catholic, as the Viscounts Clare had done. Sometimes the predilections of the humble, such as her grandfather, could be seen prefigured in one or other of the splendid, prominent O'Briens. Sir Edward O'Brien, the second baronet, seems to have been passionately involved in the horse-racing world. He had a training ground at Dromoland, kept race-horses, had them painted, gave them delightful names like Polly Peachum, and even went so far as to have the name of a village changed to Newmarket-on-Fergus, after Newmarket in England. He seems to have been a thorough-going eighteenth-century blood, living for enjoyment. He was the son of Catherine Keightly and came into his inheritance very young.

Such was the magnificent clan with which, by implication, Kate O'Brien's grandfather claimed kinship when he had the crest of the O'Briens set up on the roof-ridge of his house. His distinguished granddaughter was partly amused and partly embarrassed by these pretensions. Nevertheless, sometimes she used to allow herself to remind me that the Hickeys and Clancys had been respectively mere hereditary physicians and Brehon lawyers to the O'Briens — the point being that my mother was a Hickey and my paternal grandmother a Clancy.

But to return to our Irish children and the course of Irish History. If any such child were to go on to read the history of the nineteenth century in Ireland, he or she would see the first part of the century as peppered with new excitements and new horrors, the excitement of the campaign for and the winning of Catholic Emancipation, the horror of the Great Famine of 1847 and all its aftermath of disease and desolation, emigration and the shrinking of the population from eight millions to five millions. In comparison, the second half of the century seems dull and muddled, given over to rural agitation, the Land War, open struggle between landlord and tenant, the Plan of Campaign, evictions, boycotts, riots, imprisonments and murders. Not until the end does full-scale drama re-assert itself, with the tragic fall from fame and glory of Parnell, and his death a year afterwards.

Behind the apparent continued penury and misery, however, life actually improved in the nineteenth century for the ordinary Irishman. There were fewer farm labourers, less division of land, and the change from tillage to grazing that had occurred in the middle of the century meant for those who survived a raised standard of living. Trade improved: people engaged in commerce could aspire to live comfortably; and if they were in wholesale business, to live with some splendour. Even on the land there was a greater integration of poor tenants into the commercial livestock economy of the century. The number of sheep in Connaught almost doubled between 1847 and 1876. At Ballinasloe Fair the price of first-class wethers rose by more than fifty per cent between the 1840s and the 1870s and the average price of first-class ewes by almost eighty per cent. Wages rose by at least fifty per cent and in some places doubled between the 1840s and the late 1860s. After the introduction of the Land Act of 1881 the arbitration of rents was provided for, and the Act empowered the Land Commission to lend up to three-quarters of the purchase price to any tenant who wanted to buy out his holding: the loan was repayable over thirty-five years at five per cent. Not all landlords were bad landlords. The fourth Earl of Lucan, for instance, helped his tenants to buy out their land at considerable cost to himself. Not all landlords were absentees, nor wanted to live in England. Lately, we heard Molly Keane, the author of *Good Behaviour* (1981), tell us in an interview on television (1 November 1983) that her father said he would rather be shot in Ireland than live in England. The Wyndham Act of 1903 made it possible to bridge the gap between the price most landlords were ready to accept and the price most tenants were ready to pay. It provided the landowner with the bonus of twelve per cent, paid out of Irish revenue. By the early twenties of this century nearly two-thirds of Ireland's total land area had ceased to be the property of landlords.

Life improved in other ways also. The coming of the railways made travel much easier and quicker, the outlying parts of the country much more accessible; and, for those who invested in them, the railways were very profitable. Education became available to

Catholics again: in addition to the system of National Education, various orders of both male and female religious opened schools for boys and girls, while the establishment of the Queen's Colleges in Belfast, Cork and Galway provided a university education for many who otherwise could never have aspired to it. In astronomical circles the name of Ireland became famous when the third Earl of Rosse built the largest telescope in the world at Birr Castle and brought some unexpected features of the heavens into view for the first time. Here we have an instance of a landlord and the workers on his estate co-operating in a scientific experiment.

It is not, of course, possible to pretend that all was progress in the nineteenth century or that agrarian crimes and outrages did not happen. In April 1882 there occurred a particularly heinous instance. A Mrs. Henry Smythe of Dublin, on a visit to her brother-in-law, Mr. Barlow Smythe, of Barbavilla House, Co. Westmeath, was assassinated in mistake for him, as they drove back from church. Mr. Barlow Smythe had spent his whole life at Barbavilla, working for and among his tenants. For fifty years, until a few days previously, he had not ejected anyone; and this recent ejection was of a man who rented a large farm but refused for years to pay rent. Mrs. Smythe had taken a seat with its back to the horses, leaving the forward-facing seats to the elderly Mr. Barlow and Lady Harriet Monk, another member of the house-party. Mrs. Smythe's seat was one that would normally have been occupied by a man and the murderers had assumed Mr. Barlow Smythe to be in it; within a few yards of the house Mrs. Smythe's brains were blown out. The news of this terrible murder spread all over the world, and because the victim was a woman, excited more horror even than that of Sir Frederick Cavendish, which was soon to follow.

The farmer who refused to pay rent was said to have an 'association' behind him. This could have been the Fenians, or the Ribbonmen, or the Whiteboys, or Captain Moonlight, the exploits of all of which had so affected Kate O'Brien's aunts, long removed though they were from the world and safe behind their convent walls. The members of these secret societies killed not only the 'foreign' landlord but also their own 'boycotted' neighbours; yet some Irish historians defend them. P.S. O'Hegarty in his *History of Ireland since the Union* writes:-

If they fought with masks, with blunderbusses, behind hedges, with sticks and stones, with the torch to the thatch very frequently, with their political leaders and their Church against them, they fought for Right and for this Nation of ours.[2]

Mercifully there were other ways of fighting, and as the century wore on, increasingly this took place in the British Parliament. A great constitutional Irish leader arose in Parnell and an equally great English one in Gladstone, whose conscience impelled him to start rectifying British injustice in Ireland, and whose various Land Acts began the process which returned the land of Ireland to the people. I was greatly puzzled as a child by the two small busts of Gladstone in my grandmother's house. I thought them very ugly and totally unnecessary. No doubt there were similar busts in houses all over the country, as a tribute to the Englishman who was ready to promote Home Rule and actually did begin the work of dismantling the Union.

Trade, as I have already said above, improved in the nineteenth century, and successful wholesalers could not only acquire considerable wealth, but in the process become people of importance in the political and social life of their town. One such family in Limerick were the O'Maras who founded a bacon-curing firm. They were of Tipperary origin and came originally from Toomevara in that county. We do not know what particular incident, if any, sent the first James O'Mara on his journey from Tipperary to Limerick. He was not yet married when he set off: perhaps he was a younger son seeking his fortune. He went first to Clonmel where he married a miller's daughter, and then with his wife moved to Limerick. The advertisement for his goods used to run, 'O'Mara's Bacon and Hams. The Best in the World.' We do know what caused Kate O'Brien's grandfather, Thomas O'Brien, to leave his small-holding in county Limerick, between Bruree and Kilfinane, and move, about 1850, to the city. He was evicted and forced to find a new way of earning his living. The after-effects of the terrible famine of 1847 were aggravated by the Repeal of the Corn Laws and the subsequent whole-sale clearances of small holdings to enable the conversion from tillage to grazing. Thomas O'Brien, we might think, was one of the victims. But it seems that there was more to it than this. Grandfather O'Brien was something of a rebel and had been involved in the Rising of 1848, an abortive rebellion of the New Irelanders, confined to local skirmishes. One of the leaders of this movement was William Smith O'Brien of the Dromoland O'Briens. Whatever part Thomas O'Brien took in the affair, it was

enough to earn for him the displeasure of his landlords, the
Ashtowns and the Gasgoignes, and to cause them to evict him. As
it happened, what must have seemed a disaster then, turned out to
be a piece of good fortune. For Thomas O'Brien had a gift for
judging horse-flesh, and before long had built up a solid business,
buying and selling blood-horses. Well might his only daughter,
Anne, say years afterwards:– 'If ever there was a fortunate eviction,
wasn't it my father's?' We must assume that Thomas O'Brien was
a prudent man and had some money laid by.

We may indulge in another conjecture. Bruree, even today, is a
well-known horse-breeding part of the country, and perhaps
Thomas O'Brien in his tenant-farmer days had dabbled in the
business, or perhaps had merely had his eye trained by looking at his
or some other landlord's horses and following their fortunes. He
was not a young man when he went to Limerick: his daughter was
already engaged to be married, and it seems unlikely that he could,
as an elderly tyro, make a success of such notoriously uncertain a
means of earning a living.

At all events, we know that gradually he became an expert on the
breeding of blood-stock and established a stud farm with
thoroughbred stallions. Kate O'Brien's father, Tom, was born after
the arrival in Limerick, and by the time he was leaving his Jesuit
school, his father was building himself a fine brick villa beside his
stables and paddocks. Tom had inherited his father's flair with
horses and joined him in the business. Their field of operations
grew all the time. They mounted the cavalry officers in many
countries, supplied carriage pairs and hunters to the gentry of
England and Ireland. When the Empress Elisabeth of Austria came
to hunt in Ireland, the O'Briens mounted her, and Kate O'Brien
tells of the many signed photographs of the Empress that were
preserved in Shannon View, her uncle Mick's house outside
Limerick.

Both men were lucky, in so far as the innate gift which they
possessed answered a need of the times. The type of horse known
then as the Irish Hunter, bred by mating the best native mares to
thoroughbred stallions, now known as the Half-bred Irish, was in
great demand for military, especially cavalry, use and was widely
exported to Britain and the continent. Moreover, as the British
Empire expanded, there was a greater need for horses for all kinds
of purposes in overseas territories. In addition England, a highly

industrialised country, grew wealthier as the century wore on, and wealthy people wanted quality horses for their carriages and for hacking and hunting. At home the Royal Dublin Society succeeded in 1888 in getting a Government grant for the improvement of horse and cattle breeding: certain centres in the country were chosen, where a thoroughbred stallion would stand at stud for nominated mares for a fee of £1. We know that Tom O'Brien took part in this scheme; for in 1895 he is registered as owner of the thoroughbred stallion, Walmsgate: by then the service fee had risen from £1 to £5. In 1909 we find him in possession of what appears to have been a better stallion, Liao, which had raced and won as a two and three-year old before being retired to stud. The fee was now £9. In short, the circumstances of the time favoured the man whose business was horse-breeding. Kate O'Brien's grandfather, after settling in Limerick, was not active in Irish politics, but he derived much ironic pleasure from imposing his revenge on the English for that long-ago eviction by extracting from them large sums of money in return for his superb blood-horses.

Kate O'Brien's father became almost as well known in England as in Ireland. He attended the great horse fairs of Horncastle and Howden, held two annual sales at Leicester, supplied coaching colts to Messrs Wimbush, the great London jobmasters, and passed something like a thousand hunters through his hands in the course of a year. It was considered a great advantage that he knew how to ride and could 'throw his leg' over any hunter he felt inclined to buy.

People of this rising middle class ran complicated households in big houses, with standards different from the county houses, but as exacting in their own way, and it required several servants and retainers to keep a large family warmed and fed, furniture dusted and polished, young children bathed, dressed and generally looked after. Work now utterly forgotten was repetitively necessary: for instance, stainless steel had not yet been invented, and knives and forks had to be cleaned and polished after every meal with brick-bat and whiting. Great iron ranges had to be blackleaded, feather mattresses to be shaken and turned every morning. Scones were baked every afternoon, sponge-cakes regularly whipped up, jam made in due season and in some houses butter made once or twice a week. I remember in my grandmother's house one year she burnt nothing but turf, and there was a boy for bringing it into the house and for running on errands. My grandmother had a dairy separate from the house where great pans and crocks of milk gathered cream for the churning: all the vessels used in the dairy had to be scalded regularly. Hens were kept and had to be fed and shut in for the night. Cooking was taken very seriously and the preparation for a meal always seemed to me to constitute high drama, the maintaining of an even temperature in the oven requiring nice judgement and constant attention.

I imagine the kind of meals served in my grandmother's house differed little from those served in Boru House; for when Kate O'Brien was first invited to lunch in my mother's house and the main dish happened to be stuffed pork steaks, she was surprised, she said, for she had thought that it was only in Limerick that one got stuffed pork steaks. On another occasion, when we had roast beef, with Yorkshire pudding done under the joint, she said she had not had Yorkshire pudding cooked like that since she had had it in Boru House.

Servants, of course, were readily available and very cheap: all labour, in fact, was cheap and plentiful. I have an account book, dating from 1901, belonging to my maternal grandfather's building firm in Birr, County Offaly: in it are entered the wages paid to workmen and craftsmen. A labourer earned two shillings a day, a carpenter four shillings and four pence, a painter four and eight pence, a plasterer five and five pence. To try to realize the value of two shillings then in relation to values today is very difficult: we can get some idea by remembering that in the middle of the previous century a labourer would earn two shillings a week and also by considering how cheap every commodity was before the First World War in comparison with today. Sand cost a shilling a load, a two-pound loaf of bread twopence, apples a penny a dozen, a 'poke' of caramels a penny, whiskey twopence a glass. Still it must be supposed that even then whiskey was a luxury, and no matter how one multiplies two shillings a day to find today's equivalent, it would hardly stretch to luxuries. I am afraid our labourer did not get much stuffed pork steaks: he would have had to be content with crubeens.

Maids were, comparatively speaking, better off than labourers. They were paid five shillings a week, but they had board and lodging, and if 'young ladies', rather than mere girls, were part of the household, they could come in for last year's blouses and skirts. Even so, the contriving of luxuries required some ingenuity. I remember a maid of my grandmother's, called Ellen, whose cheeks were always of a bright poppy-red colour. Nature had not so endowed her. Her cheeks were rouged in an original manner. She used to buy what were called pass-books, small, penny note-books with shiny red covers: the rouge was manufactured and applied by spitting on the covers and rubbing the resulting liquid on her cheeks. I was interested, because she gave me the inside pages to scribble on. My mother was worried about her poisoning herself, but never dared to bring up the subject. Ellen was formidable in her own way, and had a very high opinion of herself: she was merely a 'cook-general' with my grandmother, but had been cook proper in several of the county houses round about. She used to walk out with some of the soldiers from the barracks, and once sent me out by the wicket-gate to tell the soldier who was waiting for her that 'Cook says she is very sorry but she can't go out with you tonight'. I was to be sure to say 'Cook' and not 'Ellen'. I remember being worried, because I was a shy child, and also because I did not think my mother would approve, if she knew of the transaction. Ellen frequently told us that she was 'the best cook Corolanty' (one of the 'big' houses) 'ever had'. She read to us, played cards with us, baked delicious sponge cakes for us and told us the scandals of the town. We spent more time with her than with the grown-ups of the family. If this were so in a family like ours, with an energetic mother in charge, the O'Brien children could have been no strangers to the commerce of the kitchen, at least after their mother's death and during the school holidays.

Kate O'Brien mentions more than once the gaiety of Limerick, a garrison town, with young officers eager to enjoy themselves, and townspeople ready to entertain and be entertained. She is writing about the closing years of the last century and the beginning of this. But the Edwardian after-glow lasted a long time in Ireland, even during the war and for some years afterwards. I was a child in the second decade of the century and I remember telling Kate O'Brien that it seemed to me then that grown-ups did nothing but enjoy themselves, go to race meetings, play tennis and golf, have bridge evenings and musical evenings, not to talk of endless tea-parties. I found it very boring. I was a strenuous-minded child and thought that people should be exploring the North Pole, throwing bridges across great gulfs, penetrating darkest Africa or the untrodden banks of the Amazon, fighting for lost causes and leading down-

hearted troops to unexpected victory, like St. Joan of Arc; or if they
must play tennis, at least perform at Wimbledon. Kate O'Brien said
that, on account of going to boarding school so young, she did not
see so much of the social doings of her elders at a very tender age as
I obviously had done, but what she had observed had not bored
her, though it often puzzled her, that I must have been an absurd
child, and clearly a militarist. Clearly, what Kate O'Brien was
doing was already studying human society as it is, and not as one
might think it ought to be.

Limerick, like the town of my childhood, was an hospitable
place, and Kate O'Brien mentions not only the frequent visits of her
mother's relations to Boru House, but also the customers from
England who came on business and were invited to stay. The old
traditional rules of Gaelic — and of Anglo-Irish — hospitality lasted
well into the beginning of this century. Crofton Croker, in his
Researches in the South of Ireland, writes:-

These hovels have been already described; yet miserable and destitute of
comfort as they are, the benighted peasant or houseless mendicant, who
raises the latch with the benediction, 'God save all here!' is confident of
receiving shelter and every rite of hospitality as far as it is in the power of
the inmates to bestow them. He is welcomed to the best seat the cabin
affords, the largest potato is selected from the dish and placed before him,
and that 'reserve towards strangers which alike characterize the
Englishman and his mastiff', is unknown.[3]

The fourth Earl of Kingston, who built Mitchelstown Castle,
often had as many as a hundred guests at a time staying with him.
Joyce Cary tells us of Cromwell House, an Irish house, as it were,
transported to the suburbs of London, the home of his great uncle,
Tristram, who became the head of the family on the death of Cary's
grandfather, a house where all the grand-nephews and nieces
gathered as of right, as they would have done if the family still lived
in Ireland, where even cousins had the entrée, and were given hospitality and money if they needed it. In my grandmother's house, too,
the guest was sacrosanct. If possible, one anticipated a guest's
wishes; but if anything unforeseen was required, it was supplied at
once. I remember a remote cousin of my grandmother, a Mrs.
Dunne, who used to come on a visit from time to time. She owned
a precious relic of the Dominican saint, Fr. Vincent Ferrer: it had
been handed down in her family from the Penal days, and was said

to have been given by a fugitive priest to some ancestor, in gratitude for rescue or comfort. Mrs. Dunne used to come with her relic for a laying-on of hands, so to speak. I suspect that when she grew tired of her own house and felt like a little change, she went on a series of visits with the relic, knowing that it made her more than usually welcome anywhere. On one occasion in our house the weather became very cold — it was November — and though Mrs. Dunne had a stone hotwater bottle in her bed and an eiderdown over her, she declared that she was cold at night, that she was used to a grandchild in her bed and might she have one of us instead? Consternation struck all of us. Mrs. Relicky Dunne, as we called her, could not be refused her request, we knew, but we waited with drawn breath to see whom she would choose. Luckily the choice did not fall on me, but on the sister next to me in age. Though I knew the rules, I was a rebellious child, and no power on earth would have got me into Mrs. Relicky Dunne's bed. I should have disgraced myself and my grandmother's house. My sister, then as afterwards, was of a different disposition; like the Chinese, she believed in 'suiting self to circumstances', and reluctant but polite, she spent some nights as substitute grandchild in Mrs. Dunne's bed. If a similar request had been made in Kate O'Brien's father's house, the result would have been the same, and 'no questions asked and no complaints allowed', so she said, when I told her this story.

Kate O'Brien was born in Limerick on the third of December, 1897, the last of four girls in a family of nine. She was preceded by her sisters, May, Clare and Nance and by her brothers Jack, Michael and Tom. Two brothers, Eric and Gerard, followed. She was born into an Ireland enjoying, as we have seen, a period of comparative prosperity and into a family well able to live in ease and comfort, employ servants to wash and starch the damask-linen tabelcloths of the day, put good food on its mahogany or rosewood tables, educate its children at the best schools of the neighbourhood, transplant the whole family to the seaside for the summer (the virtues of iodine-laden sea-air were highly regarded at the time) and dress its ladies in the finest silks and merinos from Switzer's or Arnott's of Dublin. I heard a salesman in a Galway shop say to Kate O'Brien when she was ordering some household goods for her house in Roundstone:- 'What would have been good enough for Boru House will do, I suppose, Miss O'Brien?'

Kate O'Brien always spoke of Boru House as an ugly red-brick

house, but it was roomy and easy to run, and for her grandfather it
had been a declaration of his wealth and standing in the community.
It was also, by virtue of its name and the emblazing of the O'Brien
arms, an assertion of a claim to aristocratic blood. Perhaps it had
been the name of William Smith O'Brien, as much as abstract
patriotism, that had led her grandfather into the affairs of the New
Irelanders?

Certainly Kate O'Brien, when she chose, commanded all the
aptitude for boredom and hauteur any aristocrat could desire. She
did not suffer fools gladly. She expected people to be what she called
'agreeably civilised'. She thought a certain amount of flattering attention her due, and she had what Chesterton called the 'great social
talent for being tired'. She lost interest very quickly and made no
attempt to hide the subsequent exhaustion. 'Merely not to be bored
is such a relief' she would say. She found most people's ways of
entertaining themselves inexplicable. 'It is pitiful', she often said,
'what people will do to amuse themselves, pitiful.' As she grew
older she made magisterial pronouncements which there was no
answering or capping. I remember, when the sister mentioned
earlier died after an illness of many years and I would find myself
crying at all kinds of inconvenient moments, instead of consoling
me in the usual way, she would say:– 'I have made a study of grief
and the best people always cry.' Once I told her in a letter about a
friend's sealyham which had given birth at a great age to her first
puppies and had kept the whole household awake all night as she
travailed. In her reply she wrote:– 'What you tell me about Doreen's
sealyham is very interesting: it just goes to show how careful we all
ought to be as we advance in age and folly.' She could use such a
technique to be charmingly humorous or utterly crushing.

Kate O'Brien's mother's people, the Thornhills, from Kilfinane,
were of Cromwellian stock, but this particular branch had quickly
been assimilated into the native Irish, becoming Catholics in the
second generation and having much difficultly, as a consequence, in
holding on to their land. Her grandfather Thornhill, she tells us, did
not live on either of his large farms, but kept a shop in Kilfinane and
lived there: this, she conjectures, was the result of complications
about land tenure. She attributes the good looks of her family to the
Thornhills, but her type of colouring, pale skin, dark hair, and
blazing blue eyes, is commonly regarded as a characteristic type of
Celtic colouring, and would seem to me to be as easily ascribed to

the O'Briens as to the Thornhills. One feature of the family type, the extraordinary deep-set eyes, is not easily accounted for by either a Celtic or Cromwellian origin. Such eyes remind one of archaic Greek statues.

Kate O'Brien's mother died in 1903 of cancer. Her youngest brother was still a baby and she herself only a little over five. Her elder sisters had been sent to Laurel Hill, the convent of a French order, the Faithful Companions of Jesus, known in Limerick as the 'French school'. Her father decided that it would be less lonely for the little girl to be with her sisters than to remain at home with the baby brothers, and so, at the unusually early age of five and a half years she became a boarder at Laurel Hill convent. She tells us in an article in *La France Libre* (December 1947) that she made a fearful scene when her father first took her to the convent, screaming and kicking and almost reducing her sisters to the same state of hysteria. But the Reverend Mother — English and considered to be very cold — told her that since they had never before had so small a pupil in Laurel Hill, they had had to order a special small chair for her: three of them had been sent on approval and were in the parlour, waiting for her to choose which one she would prefer. By this clever move Reverend Mother overcame the child's natural fear of her new surroundings, and Kate O'Brien began her long and happy association with the nuns of the Faithful Companions of Jesus, who from 1903 to 1916 ruled not only her spiritual life but also the thousand and one details of her ordinary daily life. The pupils at Laurel Hill were astonishingly well-fed, she tells us — and even moderately good food in an Irish Convent would be surprising enough — perhaps because the Foundress of the Order had come from Lyons, but more probably because the lay sisters in charge of the kitchen were still French.

Discipline was strict and scholastic standards were high at Laurel Hill, but inevitably so young a child as Kate O'Brien became something of a school pet. To be singled out in any way as a child gives one a sense of being special. This happens to every intelligent child, but to be special because of several reasons is to have one's identity and importance high-lighted to no small degree. Kate O'Brien was 'spoiled', as we say in Ireland, in this way, however austere she may have found life in other respects. When she went to live in England, she was regarded as an Irish charmer, and the 'spoiling' continued. A natural imperiousness of temperament was not discouraged by this treatment.

In *Presentation Parlour* (1963) she tells us how much she learnt from visiting her aunts in their convent, from watching as a 'mere and small and uninformed crowd-actor' the play of affection and rivalry, expectation and disappointment, the intricacies and involutions of human feeling that were revealed when the whole family gathered in the parlour of the convent where two of her mother's sisters were nuns. We may deduce that her own boarding school offered a similar, though more extended theatre for the sensibilities of the small watching child. To be for so long the youngest at school gave her an unrivalled opportunity for studying her elders at leisure.

The aunts in their convent were all the more demanding of and anxious about these children, because their mother was dead. However conscientious a mother is, there are long spells when she takes her children for granted. These aunts, Aunt Mary and Aunt Fanny, it seems were in a constant state of anxiety about the motherless children, who were always expected to look well and happy and physically unblemished. A sprinkling of freckles on the white skin caused consternation. 'The child is destroyed', her Aunt Fan would say. No wonder the child, grown-up, remembered the mood of the convent parlour, where sensibility so clearly got the upper hand of sense. Nuns who have themselves renounced the vanities of the world can expect the most assiduous attention to them from those remaining 'outside'.

Christmas seems to have been the time when visits to the Presentation Parlour were most frequent and protracted: the other two aunts, Aunt Annie on a visit from Fermoy, and Aunt Liddy, Uncle Mick's wife, would be there, and their father, with all his Christmas mail on show. Presents were displayed and presented. Songs and recitations and piano pieces would be called for. Vast quantities of cake and mince-pies were consumed and clothes criticized. Other visitors came and went but still the O'Brien children in their best clothes and on their best behaviour were imprisoned in the parlour where 'one false step was ne'er retrieved'.

Sensibility — indeed, hyper-sensitiveness — to family feeling remained strongly implanted in Kate O'Brien all her life. I remember when I first met her, famous, long removed from Ireland, intellectually independent, out of sympathy with a great deal that had developed in the country during her absence, how surprised I was to find her still so emotionally involved with her family, so anxious not to upset or disturb her sisters, how determined, especially, to do them all credit in Limerick. Those years of cutting a good figure in the eyes of her convent-enclosed aunts had left an indelible mark.

In the summers the O'Brien children used to be taken to the pleasures and freedom of the seaside. Their father rented a 'lodge', as the houses for letting were called, in Kilkee, in country Clare, and there the delights of the sea, the beach and the fresh air were to be enjoyed for two whole months. Their father did not stay all the time; he spent weekends with them. The eldest girl of the family, May, was in charge, and ran the holiday house, as she had done the house in Limerick since her mother's death. Kate O'Brien wrote of the delights of 'magical' west Clare many times directly, and indirectly in *The Land of Spices* (1941), *The Last of Summer* (1943), and *The Flower of May* (1953). The very journey to Kilkee was an adventure; for the last part of the journey had to made on the narrow-gauge West Clare railway, celebrated in Percy French's ballad:-

> Are ye right there, Michael? Are ye right?
> Do ye think that we'll be there before the night?
> Ye've been so long in startin
> That ye couldn't say for sartin - -
> Still ye might now, Michael, so ye might . . .
>
> Kilkee! Oh, you'll never get near it!
> You're in luck if the train brings you back,
> For the permanent way is so queer,
> It spends most of its time off the track.

But get to Kilkee the O'Brien children always did for the long, entranced summer holidays. Their anxious, loving father used to send telegrams from whatever town to which business took him. He always ended with the same words:- 'Post me all news. Fondest love, father.' One day in some small country town, he heard one post-office girl say to the other:- 'Here comes Fondest Love.' He was a loving, generous, conscientious and careful father, who wanted his children to have every advantage and grow up well-versed in the middle-class conventions. He would not allow them to go to midnight Mass on Christmas Eve in St. John's Cathedral — 'the riff-raff of the town was loose at that hour', he said, 'and his children might pick up germs or fleas'. So they had the 'bleak rigours of ordinary morning Mass, fasting and frozen'. We can suspect that in his anxiety for the family as a whole, the individual's sensibilities and need for privacy might be too little considered. All the Christmas morning post, for instance, had to be shared by all, the aunts in the convent included. But this was not uncommon in Irish families of the time. Perhaps it is not uncommon in any kind of family at any time.

In the summer of 1907, the year of the World Exhibition, some of the O'Brien children, instead of going as usual to Kilkee, were sent to stay for a few weeks with their Aunt Anne Hickey in Dublin. This aunt was married to a man, like their father, in the horse-trading world. They lived, in some splendour, in 39 Mespil Road, in the house that afterwards belonged to Miss Iris Kellett and from which, until she moved to county Kildare, she conducted her Riding School. The Exhibition bored Kate O'Brien, Kitty, as she was then called, but she liked Mespil Road, with the leafy stretch of the canal between Baggot Street and Leeson Street bridges, the boys swimming in the water and the bursts of clapping from Fitzwilliam Tennis Club on the other side. She was to put her early experience of Dublin to use when she set *The Flower of May* in the house in Mespil Road in the year of the Exhibition. Looking back, however, from the standpoint of her own life, Kate O'Brien was inclined to regard these summer weeks in Dublin as a period of exclusion from the 'Paradise' of Kilkee.

In spite of her mother's death, therefore, because she had this loving father, anxious to secure every possible advantage for his children, and affectionate, protective, elder sisters, Kate O'Brien's life as a child was not unhappy. She seems, indeed, to have enjoyed her childhood and to have been much indulged at home and at school. She liked school, was very industrious and an omnivorous reader. She tells us in an article in *University Review* (Vol III No 2) how astonished she had been in her first year in University College Dublin to be summoned to the President's office and warned that, if she did not attend First Arts lectures in Irish, she would not be allowed to sit the examination. She had to be given a second warning; for she had not taken the first one seriously: 'I had been spoilt in school where no one had ever suggested that I could in any circumstances be barred from any academic trial that I proposed to myself.' The Bishop of Limerick himself, the redoubtable Edward

Thomas O'Dwyer, had taken an interest in her progress. 'He was a man with an unexpected regard for the brains of women.'

Kate O'Brien's father died in June 1916 and family circumstances, as so often on the death of a father, were radically changed. She had not only to face the natural grief of such a bereavement but uncertainty about her future. She won a county council scholarship on the results of her final school examinations that summer, but some members of her family felt that the most prudent course would be for her to secure immediately a 'nice safe job', in a bank, for instance, like that proposed for Anna in *The Land of Spices* by her grandmother. Not many people at the time had a regard for the brains of women: it was still taken for granted that girls would marry and that they needed only to mark time until their particular 'Prince Charming' appeared, swept them off their feet and planted them in the road their mothers had properly taken before them. Even in my generation this still lingered on. I remember an uncle writing to congratulate me on my B.A. and adding facetiously 'I am wondering whether the next step will be M.A. or Ma.' Enid Starkie, a contemporary of Kate O'Brien's, a Dubliner, whom, however, she did not meet until 1939, was something of an exception. Her father wanted her to go to Oxford and do well there. But this, according to Enid, constituted another kind of problem, the burden of living up to his expectations and the fear of disappointing him. Kate O'Brien, like many of her subsequent young heroines, felt the need not only of further education, but of more time before she committed herself to a career, felt no doubt within herself a sense of undefined talent and a craving for the freedom in which to grow and develop. It is a fearful thing for most young people to have to give up all other chances and choose what is to be their way in life, but for those who feel that they have some unemerged talent, some just-suspected gift, it is all but intolerable. Self-education and self-exploration are necessary to discover what it is one is precisely fitted to do, what it is that will result in one's being one's own mistress. 'The muddy lane ahead and boiled mutton on Saturday' must be avoided for as long as possible and the wide meadows and deep hedges of anticipation searched and lingered in. The necessary time was given to her. She went up in the autumn of 1916 to University College, Dublin, to read French and English for a B.A. degree. She stayed in Loreto Hall, one of the two Halls of Residence — the other being Dominican Hall — for girl students on St. Stephen's Green.

As she lay in bed in her cubicle on her first night, she heard another newcomer say suddenly to a friend:- 'Did you remember to bring cutlery, Florrie?' For some reason or another, this arbitrary expression of anxiety struck Kate O'Brien as very funny, and it became one of her catch phrases in circumstances to which one was supposed to come equipped:- 'Did you remember to bring cutlery, Florrie?'

The Dublin to which she came in autumn 1916 was still reeling physically and spiritually from the effects of the Rising in the previous spring — the shellings and burnings which laid waste the centre, the shock and horror of the execution of the leaders of the Rising, the deporting of hundreds of the rank and file to penal servitude in England, the murder of Francis Sheehy Skeffington, the execution of Roger Casement. The public were filled with gloom and uncertainty: the winds were bitterly cold. Kate O'Brien never liked Dublin much: she found it a perishing cold place, nor did the opulence of some of its wealthier suburbs please her: she detested the annual ebullience of almond and cherry blossom in Ailesbury Road for instance.

But in what, since 1908, had become University College, Dublin, still mainly sited on St. Stephen's Green in numbers 85 and 86, once the home of the Catholic University, and still pondering on its first Rector, Cardinal Newman's *The Idea of a University: Lectures on the Scope and Nature of University Education* (1852), in which he had rigorously differentiated between a seminary and a university, she found what she described as 'slap-dash' freedom. U.C.D. was, she said, a seemingly

ill-directed, or if you like, non-directed place of learning — but it was open: you could find books and wits there. There was learning and eccentricity about and an indifference in government — so that whoever wanted to, just up from the country, could run free and wild enough into the first sweet shallows of humanistic studies.[4]

From being an industrious pupil, she became a casual and sceptical student, spending most of her time in idle chat with her fellows. And, of course, for her, as for James Joyce and his contemporaries before her, and for generations of students after her, including my own, there was the marvellous, the unique National Library, unique, not so much for the books it provided but for the reading-room which, with its green-shaded lights, seemed more like a room set apart in a temple than in a library, providing a place absolutely free from interruptions or distractions, if one chose, or, if one chose otherwise, serving as a club where one could count on meeting one's friends.

On the whole, Kate O'Brien took her official duties as a student rather lightly, as we can see from the episode of the non-attendance at First Arts Irish lectures, but she did well, nevertheless, in that and her subsequent B.A. examination, though she was greatly disappointed with her Second-class Honours results. The English Professor, the Jesuit Father George O'Neill, thought he had another Alice Meynell in her, she tells us, and tried to encourage her to write poetry, but she knew herself that the only kind of poem she would ever write would be a thoroughly bad one, and her witty, unkind fellow-students thought so too. The poet, Austin Clarke, then a young lecturer in the English Department, arrested her attention and from him she could get light and useful direction: she was duly gratified when he announced that he found in one of her essays 'the outward sign of inward grace'.

But it was the French Professor, Roger Chauviré, who arrived in U.C.D. only in Kate O'Brien's last year there, who revealed the study of literature as a serious adult occupation, its practice as an 'exact and exacting skill, a form of lovely science'. Listening to him lecturing on seventeenth and eighteenth-century poetry, she 'grew up', she tells us. I can well believe her; for when I was a student in U.C.D., Roger Chauviré was still exercising his skill: his students looked forward to his lectures as the highlight of the week, and I, who was not reading French for my degree, envied them their good fortune. French literature and French life continued to interest and influence Kate O'Brien. For her Flaubert was the greatest novelist in the nineteenth century, France the European country where intellectuals and writers were taken for granted, as much a part of life as the green-grocer, the baker and the haberdasher, French cooking not to be spoken of in the same breath as other kinds of cooking.

Her time in U.C.D., in addition to providing her with a respectable degree, afforded her that pause, that rest from the necessity to settle immediately on a way of earning her living, that opportunity for considering her talents and where they might lead her, which she had seen as essential at the end of her school days. It gave her congenial companions, friends for life, some of them, like Violet

Connolly, Veronica Turleigh, and Kathleen Cunningham, who
afterwards returned to U.C.D. as Professor of German. It was
Kathleen Cunningham who said that she felt she had been addressed
as 'Dear Reader' by greater writers than Alice Meynell.

But U.C.D. does not seem to have readily suggested to her how
she was to earn her living. She took her degree in the autumn of 1919
but at the beginning of 1920 we find her staying with her Aunt
Annie in Fermoy, putting off the moment when she would have to
go to England and, in her own words, 'choose a job', not find, but
choose one. In the summer of that year she went to London, where
her sisters, May and Clare, already lived. She did some free-lance
journalism, reviewing for *The Sphere*, under the genial editorship of
Clem Shorter. But she soon found a much better opening, a job in
the foreign language department of *The Manchester Guardian Weekly*
where she worked for the great editor, C.P. Scott. She was paid £5
a week, a princely sum for the time. But *The Manchester Guardian
Weekly* soon afterwards decided to discontinue its page on foreign
papers, and her job went with it. She moved back to London,
where she taught from January 1921, for the first half of the year, in
St. Mary's Convent, England's Lane, Hampstead. She was so
beautiful at the time, it seems, that the school became all but
unmanageable with *schwärmerei*. But, that aside, she had hardly the
temperament for teaching, for the repetitive slog and the endless
exercise of patience. In fact she was to say in an interview after the
success of her play that she hated teaching. She did not return in the
autumn; instead she went with her sister, Nance, and her brother-
in-law, Stephen O'Mara, to the United States. She was needed,
partly as a companion for her sister, who was not very well at the
time, and partly as secretary for her brother-in-law who was in
America on political business, to organize the raising of a loan for
de Valera. She enjoyed her stay in the United States but returned
with Nance and Stephen in 1922.

The previous year in London she had met a Dutchman, Gustaaf
Renier, who wanted to marry her. She always spoke of marriage as
an undertaking of desperate gravity — as indeed it is, for all that it
is a common event — and quite clearly she was not ready for it; for
she left London and Gustaaf and went to Spain, to the village of
Santurco on the Viscayan coast outside Bilbao, as a 'Miss', to teach
the children of the wealthy de Areilza family. In the novel, based in
Spain, which was to emerge from her time there, she had the

heroine, Mary Lavelle, fall in love with a Spaniard. What Kate O'Brien did was to fall in love with Spain: she was to love it for the rest of her life. In a paper which she read to the Spanish Society in U.C.D. in 1963, she said:-

Bilbao was and is a dark and formidable town — full of frowning banks and counting houses, with a great dirty river, and terrible poverty, terrible slums. A centre of great concentrated wealth and also indeed the heart of the Basque Nationalist movement. A city of strong individuals and much character . . . Here certainly was not any Spain an idle girl might have dreamt up — but I found it very interesting — and very shocking . . . Ten years later I returned as an ordinary traveller — and then I think that for most of the summers of 33, 34, 35 — until the Spanish War broke out in July 1936 — I used to fool about the cities of Castile. Taking my time and spending little money. I was fascinated and very happy.[4]

Her tribute to Spain was the travel-book, *Farewell Spain*, written after the outbreak of the Spanish War, and published in 1937. In it she tells us that it was in Spain as a 'Miss' that she began to attempt to write.

All this chopping and changing of jobs, this travelling and moving around, with Ireland as a point of reference, means, of course, that Kate O'Brien had not yet found her way in life. It also means that she was storing up impressions, registering character, temperament and events in the manner of the born observer, of the writer, for future use. In 1923 she was back in London, having decided to marry Gustaaf Renier. The ceremony took place in the Registry Office of Hampstead on 17 May 1923. The marriage was witnessed by two Dutch friends of her husband, and both he and his new wife describe themselves as journalists, a description which more accurately tells what she thought of herself than the facts at the time.

Probably Kate O'Brien could already have said of herself what many years later she ascribes to Matt Costello in *Pray for the Wanderer* (1938):-

He believed in impulse, pursuit and danger; high fences and blind riding; the courage to race life as it flies. It was because of all these faiths that his greatest faith was in personal liberty — a faith that had finally driven him out of the Church, but which made it impossible for him to find any resting place in contemporary life.[5]

So in pursuit of high fences and blind riding, she married Gustaaf. It was a very short and stormy relationship, lasting just eleven months. She used to joke, if one asked her why she left her husband, and say it was because he counted the strawberries:- 'one for you, one for me, two for you, two for me, etc.' In other words, she was suggesting it was a case of incompatibility of temperament, a phrase then coming into vogue, he neat and careful, she impulsive and extravagant. There were also difficulties about the particulars of housekeeping. As the son of a Dutch mother, he expected meticulous standards of cleanliness. She, reared in a convent, at home the youngest of four girls, with servants to do the housework, just back from living in Spanish grandeur, with the best will in the world did not know how to keep a house clean. The uses of Vim were unknown to her until she asked her eldest sister, May, how to clean a greasy sink.

In any event Kate O'Brien did not intend to spend the rest of her life keeping anybody's sink clean. She did not yet know, perhaps, what she wanted to do, but she appears to have had little doubt about what she did not want to do: marriage and housekeeping were not for her, and within a twelvemonth she was once again a free agent. Her marriage seems to have been no more than a passing incident in her career. It is clear from Gustaaf Renier's letters to her sister, Nance, at the time that he did not want the marriage to end. He wrote:- 'Kitty says she has never been happy with me, that she is not made for matrimony and cannot live with me under false pretences.' In after-life she spoke amiably but lightly about her ex-husband. For his part, he was to acquire quite a reputation for his book, *The English, are they Human?*

When Kate O'Brien came to her true vocation, everything in her past life was to become grist to her mill and to serve her in one way or another — school-days, time spent abroad, life in Ireland, England, France, Spain and the United States. In the Easter holidays of 1921, for instance, she went to Belgium with the French Mistress from the Convent in England's Lane and saw the original of the convent that she was to use as the Mother-House of the teaching Order depicted in *The Land of Spices*. She had become what Henry James advised the aspiring writer to be, 'one of those people on whom nothing is lost'.

After leaving her husband, she worked as secretary and publications editor for the Sunlight League, editing the occasional publication, which appeared when they could afford to print it. While she was doing this, a friend from her U.C.D. days, Veronica Turleigh, by then a distinguished actress on the English stage, made her a bet that she could not write a play. She took up the challenge and in six weeks had written *Distinguished Villa*. It was accepted by the Repertory Players and put on at the Aldwych on Sunday 2 May 1926. The General Strike, which began the next day, meant that no notices could be published, but word of mouth went around, suggesting that here was a play that should be seen by a wider public, and on 13 July it was produced at The Little Theatre, Adelphi, The Strand. It opened to a chorus of praise, with few dissenting voices, and in spite of a heat wave, ran for three weeks. Kate O'Brien woke one morning, like Byron, to find herself famous. The play was noticed by every newspaper and journal, from *The Times* to *The People*, from *Vogue* to *Punch*.

Read today, *Distinguished Villa* strikes one as contrived in plot, with a melodramatic ending, but the author's powers of close and satiric observation are evident, and at least two of her characters are convincingly 'real', Mabel Hemworth in a horrifying, and Matty in a pathetic way. At the time it was the 'realism' that impressed, or shocked, the critics. Of all the tributes that she received the one she most valued was a telegram from Sean O'Casey saying, 'Dublin ventures to congratulate Limerick'; she remembered the message as 'Dublin salutes Limerick'.

With this success, Kate O'Brien must have felt that she had discovered what form her literary talents would take. In some of the interviews which she gave to the journalists — when they discovered where she was to be found, for she had not even left her address with the theatre — she mentioned another play which she was writing, called *The Silver Roan*, set in Ireland, and obviously concerned with the world of horses. 'It is set in the County Limerick and is all about the Limerick Horse Show and members of the family', she writes to her sister, Nance. This was never produced, but she did have another, called *The Bridge*, produced by the Arts Theatre Club on 1 May 1927. A third play, *Set in Platinum*, is mentioned at the time but not heard of afterwards. She also mentions in these interviews novels which she had attempted but had found 'very tiring'. Tiring or not, it was, however, in the writing of novels that she found her métier, and made her reputation.

Some time after the success of her plays, she began to write a novel into which, one is justified in guessing, something from *The Silver Roan* went, and on the strength of a few opening chapters, which she showed to the publishers, Heinemann's, she was taken up by them, given an advance in royalties, and told to go away and finish the work. She went to live in the village of Ashford in Kent, and gave all her attention to writing.

It was some time, however, before the results appeared. *Without My Cloak* was not published until 1931. Kate O'Brien was a slow worker. She tells us herself, in an article called *The Art of Writing*, published in *University Review* (vol III, No 4) —

. . . I work so slowly, on such long and long reflection, that were I — as so many do — to make second and third drafts, no book of mine would ever reach a publisher. No, I labour from the very beginning to get said at once, as closely as I can, what I intend to say. This makes me very slow indeed — but I am surprised and relieved afterwards at how few and trivial are the corrections I have to make — and because I am so slow, my manuscripts have for the most part a very orderly look — almost as if they were fair copies. It is one method — probably not the best — but we can only work in self-taught fashion.[6]

She also tells us in this article that she has always been visited, before she could begin to write any of her books, by a 'crisis of acceptance', an epiphany in 'which the image seen becomes the image that will be expressed'. What this image seen was in relation to *Without My Cloak* we do not know. Some moment of illumination threw its light backwards and around and made clear a pattern of family history and feeling, a family pattern that was of course rooted in the history of her country, and represents in the story of one family the general emergence of the downtrodden and persecuted native people of Ireland in the nineteenth century, out of anonymity into a position of some social success and affluence.

Kate O'Brien took, one might say, a long time getting off the ground, but once up, her flight was confident. *Without My Cloak* is an accomplished novel, showing no signs of the apprentice writer, skilful in construction, wise in its judgements, weaving the background story of a family's endurance and success as a unit with the sufferings of the heart and exposure to fate of its individual members, and ultimately indicating the sallying out unprotected into the highway of life that the title from Shakespeare suggests. The canvas is wide, covering a century of progress, from great-grandfather to great-grandson and suggesting subtle links between the horse-thief, Anthony, in his admiration for the beauty of his stolen, thoroughbred mare, and Denis with his love of beauty, expressed in the creation of the garden as a work of art. In moving from Anthony to Denis, the writer moves from the historic theme of dispossession to the modern one of alienation.

II

THE FAMILY

The opening paragraph of Galsworthy's *The Man of Property* sets before us a description of an English Victorian upper-middle class family in 'full plumage'. The witness of such a spectacle, the author tells us, could glean from a gathering of this family —

no branch of which had a liking for the other, between three members of whom existed nothing worthy of the name of sympathy, evidence of that mysterious concrete tenacity which renders a family so formidable a unit of society, so clear a reproduction of society in miniature. He has been admitted to a vision of the dim roads of social progress, has understood something of patriarchal life, of the swarming of savage hordes, of the rise and fall of nations. He is like one who, having watched a tree grow from its planting — a paragon of tenacity, insulation and success, amidst the deaths of a hundred other plants less fibrous, sappy, and persistent — one day will see it flourishing with bland, full foliage, in an almost repugnant prosperity, at the summit of its efflorescence.[1]

Kate O'Brien in *Without My Cloak* gives a more remarkable picture of a family, risen from humble beginnings to such an efflorescence, more remarkable because the family here has far more formidable obstacles to overcome, more tenacity to exhibit, more ingenuity to exercise, a greater distance to cover than the Yeomen ancestry of the Dorset Forsythes. The family here is Irish, of native stock, Catholic in religion, and had had to survive the penal laws of the eighteenth century, the great famine of the 1840s which killed or sent into exile so many other millions of fellow countrymen, the subsequent political troubles — agrarian and otherwise — of the later years of the century, the grinding poverty, as well as the diseases and mishaps to which the poor of the time were everywhere subject. The story proper is set against a short prologue which briefly pictures for us the background of a wilder, earlier Ireland, of abject poverty, deprivation, crime, and the resourcefulness of a driven people. We are given a glimpse of the horse-thief, Anthony, leading the stolen thoroughbred mare, Rose-Red, through the Gap of Storms to look for shelter in the town of Mellick, set in the Vale of Honey. Brief as it is, the prologue suggests, in the contrast between the thick-set Anthony and his beautiful Rose Red, the emergence of the flower of beauty from earthy roots.

The Irish family differs from the English one in another profound way. Instead of the lack of sympathy obtaining among the Forsythes, the Considines are only too sensitive to one another's feelings: there is an interplay of sympathy which can by reaction produce mutual irritation, or create such close fellowship that some members are rendered thereby dissatisfied with later, necessary relationships.

This makes for a more complex and, certainly, a livelier novel. No one in *Without My Cloak* is a passive character, as is Irene, for instance, in *The Man of Property*. No one lacks intelligence: no one is capable of brutality, and the family, as a family, is concerned about individual members, protects their interests, and rejoices on the whole, allowing for the odd inevitable pang of envy or irritation, in their advancements. The individual member must, however, accept the general ruling; for this family is also concerned with conserving property, with keeping up appearances and observing the conventions.

Thus, while the family nurtures, it also constricts its members, and the overall theme of *Without My Cloak* is the necessity of love for the development and well-being of every human creature, adult as well as child, and as a concomitant of this the necessity for the freedom which true love allows to the beloved. For true love embodies *agape* as well as *eros*, when it is a question of love between the sexes, and is totally *agape* where other relationships are concerned.

The women of the Considine family do not fare very well in this respect, any more than women in other novels of the time or in real life fared. Molly, beautiful and gentle, married to Anthony, the youngest, most capable and attractive of the Considine sons, is laid at the age of thirty-three in 'that preposterous place, her grave'. She died giving birth to their ninth child. Now the author makes it clear that Molly is no victim: she loves her husband and had from the beginning made her bargain with fate: if death in childbirth is the risk she has to run for her husband's love, she is prepared to take that risk. It is also made clear that Anthony is no rough beast insisting on his 'conjugal rights'. He tries to spare his wife. But neither he nor she sees any way out of the problem of their mutual attraction, given the religious teaching of their Church and their absolute acceptance of that teaching.

But, while Molly loves her husband absolutely, his love for his wife is not exclusive; and the evening that he hears from her of her ninth pregnancy is an evening when he has returned from a visit to Amsterdam and an encounter with a Dutch woman which he found so entertaining that he foresees it will not be the last. The irony resides in the bare recounting of the facts: no authorial comment is made, no obvious contrast made between the confinement of the woman and the freedom of the man. These were the facts of life: Anthony in terms of his time is a good and loving husband.

So is Jim Lanigan, husband of Caroline, the brilliantly beautiful Considine daughter, but Caroline, married to a wealthy, worthy husband for twenty years, mother of the 'six most beautiful children in Mellick', is in a far worse plight than Molly. She is bitterly unhappy, not because her husband is cruel or unkind, but simply because she does not love him, not even in the simplest erotic sense. She feels used, exploited, exhausted by her inability to respond to what for her is an arid passion, conscious of the inexorable slipping away of time and the waste of her beauty, which she cannot but be aware of. Here the author uses the Considine son, Eddie, a bachelor living in London, as authorial mouthpiece; she also uses him to illustrate, in his bond with Caroline, the kind of friendship that Caroline would have needed to find in any lover as part of his love, the gaiety and sense of ease that she required in any loving relationship. Eddie, looking on at the game, reflects that Caroline's is a simple, common problem — her husband cannot give her the sensual release he receives from her.

At the age of forty-two Caroline can stand it no longer, and on an impulse she bolts, runs away from her husband, telling him she is going to Dublin to shop, but actually travelling on to London to seek refuge with Eddie. This incident reveals the family as a cruel and restrictive power: all their skill and influence is brought into play, their resources mobilised, first to throw dust in the eyes of Mellick society and, secondly, to make certain that Caroline is brought home to her husband. Anthony is dispatched to bring her back with as little delay as possible.

In the two days of her freedom, Caroline, we are told, meets

Richard Froud, a friend of Eddie's, and falls in love with him and he with her. There is something a little fairy-tale-like about this episode, though we all know such experiences can happen, but it serves two purposes, apart from the romanticism which it imparts to Caroline's story. It shows how normal Caroline is, how attractive her character, with its complete lack of coquetry and capacity for enjoyment and it also shows, in her recoil and refusal of this proffered love, how absolutely she has been moulded by her Catholic up-bringing, how her Catholic conscience cannot throw off the doc-trines inculcated since childhood.

Here the author does intervene directly to say that if Richard Froud had made Caroline his lover, instead of allowing her to talk about her life, if she had had at last an experience of reciprocal carnal love, she would have been his happily for the rest of her life and lost to the Considines. This seems to me at least questionable. Caroline's character has not been depicted as quite as simple as that. Lost to the Considines she might well have been, but happily lost and untroubled, hardly. When the author returns to this theme, which she does in subsequent novels, the matter is not so easily resolved.

When they come for Caroline, she is ready to return, to duty and habit and 'Jim and the children', but in fact to increasing unhappiness, a steady deterioration in character and manner, becoming sharp and bitter, where once she had been gentle and gay. The love she needed as an individual, not as a member of any family, she found too late. She is to prove a source of great anxiety and trouble to Anthony's son, Denis, who admires her beauty and is puzzled by her misery. The degradation to which she descends is finally shown when she turns on Denis when he makes his bid for freedom.

Of the remaining Considine sisters, plain, sensible Teresa is married to the silly, proverb-quoting Danny Mulqueen, on whom incorporation in the family business has conferred some measure of dull usefulness. Teresa's heart is not with him. It is centred on her syphilitic son, Reggie, who has ruined his life by vicious, idle dissipation. She is one of the many Irish women who have tried to compensate themselves for an inadequate husband by lavishing all their tenderness on a son; in this instance, ironically, a son less deserving than her husband. The youngest sister, Agnes, remains unmarried, well provided for by her father, and after his death, offered a home by Anthony. She is a typical old maid of the period, with nothing but a good cry, cups of tea and eau-de-Cologne for

solace. In this she is something of a stereotype, but between them
the fates of the three Considine sisters illustrate fairly fully the
general lot of the well-off women of the time.

The love that fosters and encourages, that delights in the personality of another is not to be found here between man and woman.
But it is present in the love of Anthony for his eldest son, Denis, a
love which Anthony himself cannot account for and which the rest
of the family view with muffled scepticism and irritation, expecting
it to lead to some kind of *débacle*. *Without My Cloak* is divided into
three parts, but the third part is as long as the other two-thirds put
together and is given over to an exploration of Denis's growth to
manhood and his relationship with his father. The boy has been
born with the temperament of an artist, and through his father's
indulgent love, is happily allowed to develop this natural bent. By
the time he is eighteen Denis knows what he wants to be, a landscape
gardener, an architect of gardens, and he has crammed his father's
library with books on the history of gardening. He has, moreover,
begun to formulate a philosophy of gardening: he sees a garden as
always the outcome of a particular culture, and at the same time as
a general expression of man's need to work with nature as well as
against her. He who would be master of the art of gardening in this
sense, he tells himself, would need to have a knowledge of many
exact sciences, but also an appreciation of the liberal arts. Denis is
rapt and excited, absorbed in his pursuit, a boy who has civilised
himself beyond the standards of his society and his family.

His father has not only encouraged him in the abstract, but has
allowed him from the age of sixteen to start putting his ideas into
practice in their own garden of thirty acres. The aunts and uncles
howl in derision: his aunt Agnes is particularly infuriated. They are
all convinced that Anthony is ruining Denis by pandering to his
whims. But Anthony knows what he is doing: he intends to grapple
this most beloved son to himself by all possible hoops of affectionate
indulgence, by all the ruthless charm that is in him. He has even
abandoned the idea of a second marriage for fear of the alienating
effect it might have on Denis and had kept him at home when his
brothers were sent to boarding school. Anthony loves his son
enough to indulge his every whim, well enough to foster his
creativity. He loves him more than he loved Molly, but he does not
love him well enough to free him from an over-possessive bond: he
makes no overt demands on him, but the boy feels the weight of

unspoken emotional demands.

Here there emerges the other leading theme of *Without My Cloak*, the need for freedom within love, or, it may be, through love. Love can free the spirit, but the finding of such a love is problematical. Education, on one's own terms, is another, easier, means to freeing the spirit. This is what Denis is seeking, and like all artists, he has a horror of being tied down. At eighteen, when his school-days are over, however, he knows that he must openly declare what he is going to do in life and he knows that his father is hoping that he will settle for joining the family business. At a family luncheon party, asked suddenly by his priest-uncle:— 'What are you going to be?' — he replies: — 'But I'm going into Considine's, naturally.'

He had not been able to disappoint his father, refuse the unuttered plea that reached him from the stillness of his father's figure, arrested in his pose at the head of the table. He does his work at Considine's efficiently, but his heart is not in it. A central zest is missing from his life. He is not doing his own work, he is doing another man's work and doing it as another man wished it done. In this mood, chancing to hear that a stretch of the river Taigue is for letting, he takes it and spends his evenings in a sunken meadow by its banks, partly fishing and partly reading omnivorously.

There he meets and loves Christina Roche, illegitimate child of a scullery maid and the second son of the great house which had employed her. Christina is depicted as untutored, but as generous, beautiful, simple and noble-minded. Kate O'Brien handles the love scenes triumphantly, with the greatest delicacy. It is, as we all know, extremely difficult to describe happiness and above all the happiness of love, but the stolen, passionate, innocent, lyrical love of Denis and Christina is convincingly depicted and the hushed beauty of their nights in the little wood by the stream.

True as the feeling between them is, however, the author signals to the alert reader that this is not the ultimate experience for Denis. She introduces the oblique methods of poetry to intimate folds of meaning not yet available. Passages that might seem — however beautiful — like patches of mere decorative description, later on reveal themselves as delicately freighted with symbolic import. Before Denis first lays eyes on Christina, he sees, entranced, a single swan sweeping northwards on her lonely way up the silver stream:—

One evening of long-drawn light a swan came sweeping up the stream going northwards, past him, with the gentle tide. Denis leant out to watch her, holding himself very quiet as if she were music that he heard. The water curved ahead of her in a long, slow sweep. She took it on its crest, the track she knew. Two oars of water streamed behind her, wide and noiseless, from her folded wings. Her unstained whiteness blazed against the light that it was fleeing from, then dropped with distance into a gradual merging with the silver stream, then vanished. It was as if a ghost had passed, or was still passing. It seemed to Denis that the water that her movement had scarcely troubled held something of her now though she was gone — an echo, a trail of decoration. Where she had been had been made more lovely for ever because of her sailing past. Denis stared and saw her still, beyond his sight, taking her dreamy course to where her rest and purpose lay, her motion heavy with rest even now, her lines sharp cut in isolation and yet the whole of her at one with the warm splendour of the evening. She was alone, a northward-faring ship, but she knew her path and had turned to it because of a command in the changing light. Where was her nest? Had she found it yet, or was she still at her drowsed, unhurried navigating?[2]

Christina is not the figure the swan presages, though she may seem like it, 'as with a snapping twig' she appears. After a later meeting, leaving him, she casts a dark shadow and the distance folds her in commonplace again: there is darkness in her eyes and 'dark tracks in the grass as she moves away.'

Like almost all first loves, this love is doomed. Denis's uncle, Tom, parish priest of the region, out cooling a headache one night, overhears their parting caresses and moves into action at once. Christina is despatched, as if she were a piece of merchandise, without delay, to the United States: and if the next boat to sail were going to Australia, to Australia she would have been sent. The ruthless power of the priest and pride of family combine to remove this danger from the Considine heir.

There follows a tremendous scene of family outrage and horror, as Tom, accompanied by Teresa, arrives at Anthony's house to tell him of the disgraceful behaviour of his son and heir. All the other adult Considines happen to be gathered in the drawing-room of River Hill for an innocuous game of whist when this shock to family pride and rectitude is administered. Denis arrives to confront his uncle. Each member of the family reacts in characteristic fashion, Agnes with little yelps of spinster dismay, Sophie with downright

Kate O'Brien as a student in University College, Dublin, in 1918.

Kate O'Brien at the time she was ready to set out with her sister and brother-in-law, Nance and Stephen O'Mara, for the U.S.A. in 1921. Pictures of Kate O'Brien in a hat are very rare. She hated all hats, and in later life only wore one when attending weddings or christenings.

Facing page: Kate O'Brien as the suddenly famous author of *Distinguished Villa*, in 1926. A portrait by Sasha.

Reproduction of a portrait of Kate O'Brien by Mary O'Neill.

Facing page above: Kate O'Brien in London, 22 November 1951. On the back of this picture she wrote 'This genius, strolling in Oxford Street, desires some words of Feisal & where and how he strolls'. 'Feisal' was the name she gave the author, in return for 'Ibn Saud' for herself.
Below: Kate O'Brien and her cats, La Grise and Kelly, in the garden of The Fort, Roundstone, 1956. She is sitting on the stone seat built against the sea-wall.

Above: Kate O'Brien with her nephew, Peter O'Mara, in the garden of Strand House, Limerick, the home of her sister and brother-in-law. Facing page: In the same garden, a few years later.

Kate O'Brien with the author at a meeting of the Comunità Europea degli Scrittori, Florence, 1962.

hysterics, stunned by the information that Denis's love is an illegitimate scullery maid, Caroline with malice, Teresa with sober admonitions. Anthony, however, shocked though he is as much as the others, brings the scene to an unexpected dénouement by pretending, out of love for his son and pity for his ordeal, that he has known about the matter all along.

Denis, wrought to a white fury by his uncle's interference in his affairs, insists on being told where Christina has been sent. He follows her to New York, where, after a search lasting eight weeks, he finally comes on her by chance, only to realise that the first raptures of desire have died in him. Christina senses this from his kiss and rejects his offer of marriage:— 'she could give him what Anthony Considine would not — freedom'.

Back in Ireland, Denis spends a winter and spring of savourless and lonely days, working at the family business, but bored to exasperation and oppressed by his father's stifling love. On his twenty-first birthday, he makes an hysterical end of it. Like his Aunt Caroline, he bolts, runs away from the very midst of the official celebration by the firm. He revolts against the physical bondage of his work in the firm and against the emotional bondage of his father and family — 'Oh, God, we own one another here! What's the hell the matter with us that we insist on owning things we know nothing about?' He revolts against the sacrifice of his inner self, of his real ambitions, to the conventions of his time and place:— 'Life could only be the antithesis of death — and a brief antithesis at that — when the questing mind was free at least of its own narrow acre.' Denis wants simply to be himself, not 'a bit of a family tree'. And now, at last, he tells himself in the field by the stream where he had met Christina, he is free, free, free.

As hysteria dies in him, he knows that he must return and apologise to his father before taking the next train out of Mellick. 'Away from Mellick, round the world.' His father would now see that it had been all his own fault. At midnight he reaches the garden of River Hill exhausted, dirty, and still drunk from the unaccustomed whiskey he has been drinking, to come unexpectedly on Anna Hennessy who has escaped from the birthday dance that had gone on without Denis.

Anna, the difficult daughter of a long-established Mellick family, is in the process of being wooed by Denis's cousin, Victor Lanigan. She knows the time for his proposal has come and has escaped to the

garden to postpone the moment for as long as possible. She has not
found in Victor an answer to her expectations, the love she has read
about in the poets and that her heart tells her is a possibility, but he
has evoked a sensual response from her, and she is trying to decide
whether this will serve, whether it is all she will ever find. Denis,
who does not know Anna, as he enters the rose garden of River
Hill, sees a girl walking towards him by the stone parapet. 'She was
all in white and the dying moon poured light on her.' He is bereft
of the power to move, and her movement seems like a dream
motion, 'as once the swan had moved, he remembered, towards
Farrell's reeds.'

Denis has found his swan in human form. Anna's skin gleams
under the moon in an unbroken whiteness with her dress. She carries
her head patricianly on her curving neck. His immediate response
to her is elemental. He is undergoing that dislocation of what we
call the real world which intense emotion produces. He sees Anna
first in terms of fire:—

> *Child of light, thy limbs are burning*
> *Through the vest that seems to hide them —*

he chants to himself. Later he tells her she is drowning him, later still
that she is mad, that what is happening between them is mad. In
short, he reacts in all the clichéd ways of lovers, but in clichés made
fresh by individual experienice.[3]

As they talk, they seem to find the answer to their problems in
each other. Denis tells Anna that she must not, on any account,
marry his cousin, Victor. Anna tells Denis that he can find himself
at home as well as abroad. Asking himself if this will solve his
difficulties with his father, Denis, dishevelled and dirty, and Anna,
immaculate in white silk, sweep into the house to dance the waltz
being played by the orchestra, and nobody looking on is in any
doubt that what they are looking at is a pair of lovers.

So the novel ends on the possibility that a 'marriage of true
minds' is in the making, that *agape* and *eros* have joined hands and
that the incompatible claims of love and freedom may be reconciled.
It is an optimistic ending which will not be repeated in subsequent
novels and seems just a little too good to be true.

It is one of the few flaws in this impressive novel, written with
such a delicate understanding of the movements of the human

heart, and its insatiable longings, such a command of narrative, such a muster of characters, such sympathy for human folly, and with such a masterly evocation of the natural background to these human lives. If we may talk at all of the 'world' of a writer, Kate O'Brien's Mellick and the adjoining Vale of Honey is as distinctive as the most famous, as Hardy's Wessex, or George Eliot's Warwickshire. Rarely have the soft air, the delicate, changing light, the gentle lushness of the Irish countryside been so lyrically and so authentically interwoven with the sensibilities of the people who move through it. The voice of the great river that runs through the region tells of journeys to be undertaken, adventures to be encountered, of the mysteries of change and metamorphosis in all existence, while the claims of home and religious faith and the ambiguities of human love alternately soothe and storm the hearts of those who live near its banks.

Without My Cloak is a long, discursive novel, open to a reading as social commentary as well as an exploration of the human psyche, and a necessary exercise, we feel, for the novelist before she could take individual members of the class depicted and probe deeper into their emotional and spiritual states. She moves from the situation of the Irish family in the nineteenth century, where the combining of forces was necessary for survival, to the situation where separation is necessary for growth. For nineteenth-century Irish novelists social disadvantage was mainly historically caused. Kate O'Brien's first novel depicts Irish society at the stage where it has overcome these disadvantages, where the Irish novelist can go on to explore the perennial problems of the human condition and the war of conflicting forces within the individual spirit.

III

A GIRL AND HER CONSCIENCE

Without My Cloak won financial success and critical acclaim: in 1932 it was awarded the Hawthornden Prize. Chronicle novels were popular at the time, and the terms in which she was praised, by a fellow-chronicler, J. B. Priestley, for instance:— 'She writes well; she can create a character; she has an eye for a scene and a period' — suggest no more than the possession of the superficial talents necessary for such a *genre*. But Kate O'Brien was doing more than write a chronicle novel: she was exploring her roots, the forces that had gone to her own making and the making of many Irish families like the Considines; she was attempting to understand the world from which she had emerged. At the end of the novel she suggests a sort of fairy-tale solution for Denis, the main character, of the conflicting claims of family and individual. In her next novel, *The Ante-Room* (1934), the focus of interest is not on an external conflict: it is on an inner conflict, a conflict within the mind and soul of the heroine.

From this time on, the centre of Kate O'Brien's best novels is a heroine, or sometimes a pair of heroines. In *Without My Cloak*, Christina Roche, good girl though she is, cannot equate the abstract Christian doctrine she has been taught — that sexual love outside marriage is a mortal sin — with the actual experience of loving Denis. In *The Ante-Room* the conflict between abstraction and actuality takes a more complex form. At the end of the first novel, we heard of the splendid wedding of Marie-Rose Mulqueen, daughter of Teresa and Danny, and Vincent de Courcy Regan of Dublin. We were told moreover that Agnes Mulqueen, Marie-Rose's younger sister, had also fallen in love with Vincent. *The Ante-Room* concerns itself with this dilemma.

In *Without My Cloak* love is presented as a good in itself: without it people are the poorer: some of them, without it, show grave deterioration of character. But society never acknowledges any of this, and the manifestations of love are strictly controlled, as they are in all patriarchal societies, by Church and State, and by the modesty, considered natural, and certainly assiduously inculcated by their training, of women. The lawless manifestation of love, such as we see in Christina and Denis, though abhorrent to the Considines, could in some measure be explained by Christina's inferior social status and elementary education and the over-indulgent rearing of Denis by Anthony. Denis was only fulfilling the expectations of the aunts and uncles, who said all along that Anthony was 'spoiling that fellow'.

In *The Ante-Room* it is a carefully reared, convent-trained young girl who feels the impulses of lawless love, and a lawless love compounded by the fact that it is felt for the husband of a sister. Instead of the panoramic spread of the earlier novel, we have here a concentrated, claustrophobic probing of one relationship, confined in action to the lapse of three days. The external world, with its social and commercial activities, and the situation of the family have been established, and the author can turn her searchlight on the workings of the internal world, the movements of the loving heart and the intelligent mind in a condition of agonising conflict.

As we have seen, Kate O'Brien's young people are not troubled by puritanical scruples, nor by any Platonic sense of the discrepancy between spirit and flesh. They would claim that the flesh has its rights, and human love, in which the flesh has a legitimate part, its rights. But they have been well-trained in the doctrines of the Catholic Church and know that there are circumstances in which human love is forbidden expression. Agnes Mulqueen finds herself in such circumstances, and her conflict lies between the claims of human love and the well-trained Catholic conscience.

Agnes has been considered a plain, lanky girl when she was growing up, but now she is described as having turned out, in her sister's words, a 'tremendous beauty . . . In the poetic style, you know — like those legendary sorts of women'. This, though the Considines and their kind never underestimate, nor does the novelist, the power of beauty, especially the beauty that is 'caviar to the general', is not the point about Agnes. Her problem would have been the same had she remained plain and lanky. The point about Agnes is the spiritual crisis which she is undergoing, the conflict between clamouring love for her brother-in-law and the insistent nagging of her troubled conscience. This hidden crisis is set within the family crisis of her mother's illness.

Agnes is in charge of the household, while her mother lies dying upstairs, and the peculiar poignancy of this terminal cancer, apart from the usual and natural poignancy of all death-bed states, is that her mother is fighting to stay alive in order to continue to provide support for her beloved, syphilitic son, Reggie. Though in pain so severe that she lies most of the time drugged with morphia, she is hoping that her doctors will advise a fourth operation to prolong her life. Agnes attends to her domestic duties efficiently and mechanically, helped by the well-trained servants of the house. She will have to act as hostess to her mother's three doctors when they arrive the following day for an examination which will decide whether or not the patient is to undergo a fourth operation. She is looking forward, with as much pleasure as is possible in the circumstances, to Marie-Rose's arrival, until she is thrown into utter confusion and apprehension by the unexpected news that Vincent will accompany her sister. She loves her sister and is bound to her by all the ties of shared childhood, but all the instincts of her being as a young woman go out in love to that sister's husband.

The novel opens on the morning of All Hallows Eve, and before long Agnes's uncle, Tom, Canon Considine, arrives to suggest a triduum of prayer for the dying woman. The action of the novel is confined to the three days of prayer, All Hallowe'en, All Saints and All Souls, always a time of special devotion in the Church's calendar, and now for the Mulqueen family intended as an occasion when God's help for their mother can be fervently sought. This provides the author with an opportunity of revealing the depth and sincerity of Agnes's religious feeling. After months of absence from the sacraments, because she has been half-indulging her feeling for her brother-in-law, Agnes decides that she must go to confession, in order to be able to join the others in receiving Holy Communion for her mother's welfare. All Hallowe'en has fallen on a Sunday, so she has to make special arrangements for confession. Her examination of conscience could be taken as an abstract model of the procedure: it is rigorously honest, and she spares herself nothing, taking desolate consolation from her Jesuit confessor when he tells her that it is the fate of all human love to die. She returns home, confident in the strength of the grace she has received, and believing that now she will be able to bear the presence of Vincent with equanimity.

It needs only his hand laid on her shoulder in love to shatter her flimsy peace. Her struggle has passed through but one phase, and is to take her into deeper and darker reaches of the spirit than she could have envisioned when she left the confession box absolved.

Vincent, who woke too late to the realisation that it was Agnes, and not Marie-Rose whom he loved, is not as clearly or as convincingly presented as Agnes; he is described as a dreamer and selfish, handsome and spoiled, in a brilliant phrase, as a 'sulky god, tinkling the lustres'. He is presented through the eyes of William Curran, the local doctor, who is also in love with Agnes, senses he has a rival and dislikes the pose of the god in marble; or through the direct description of the author. His marriage to Marie-Rose is not a success: the passion that had at first bridged the differences of temperament between them no longer suffices to hold them together, and they now live a 'cat and dog's life', as Marie-Rose puts it. But, nevertheless, Marie-Rose admits to Agnes that she still wants him:— 'I don't want anyone else! That's the terrible thing. That's what makes me hate him.' So, locked in this love-hate relationship with her husband, Marie-Rose can still be hurt through him.

It is this that prevents Agnes from taking what her brother-in-law offers. On All Saints' Night she joins him at midnight in the summer house to tell him that they must not meet again for a year, that she will marry William Curran and become a useful member of society, or if Vincent cannot bear this, she will go far away and become an old maid, living in exile; but meet again, as matters stand between them, they cannot and must not. Vincent then offers the final temptation: there is another solution: they can go away together, to some old Mediterranean land where her beauty, he feels, will be sufficient excuse for any irregularity. A whole life, spent thus, passes in fantasy before his eyes, and hers: they come back to reality as if from thousands of miles of distance and years of absence. They come back to Agnes saying, 'I will never go away'. The thought of betraying Marie-Rose's trust is too much for her. So, with a final, mistaken kiss, she leaves Vincent to the frost of the November night.

What Kate O'Brien is embodying here is the Romantic conception of love as a great tragic force: that she makes the vehicle of this force an Irish girl, Catholic to the marrow in moral feeling and doctrinal training, contributes to the originality of the novel. There is not as much as a hint at edification. The battle is drawn on a field where

no purpose has been pre-determined. This gives the novel an historical dimension. Such a novel could not have been written by a native
Catholic author in the nineteenth century. Catholicism is not
presented as a characteristic of the class and race of the girl. What we
are given is Catholic feeling in its inward process, operating on the
level of the individual consciousness. Catholic teaching is not just
given mouth-service, merely acknowledged, but is understood
and accepted as an inescapable part of life. But love too is seen as
inescapable. This made Kate O'Brien's novels, in her day, accessible
to everybody in Ireland, from the maid in the kitchen to her fellow
graduates of U.C.D., and even today can cause tears to flow in
some who read her first in youth and sit down now to a re-reading.

The tragic potential of the theme is realised in the suicide of
Vincent. This, though prepared for, seems to me a mistake. Vincent's
sensibility has not been made clear to us, as Agnes's has. It is she
who is the centre of interest: his suicide has not been among the
reader's expectations: it comes as a melodramatic shock. Moreover
it seems an unnecessary cutting of the Gordian knot, a final self-
indulgence on his part, a final refusal of all love. Agnes, for her part,
finds that one kind of love, established, familial love, cannot be
sacrificed to passionate, lawless love. *Agape* has conquered *Eros*. But
even without the deterrent of her love for Marie-Rose, Agnes, we
feel, would not have taken what her brother-in-law has to offer. At
one point we find her speculating on what she would do 'if she were
free to love' him. She is not free, and never, as long as her sister is
alive, would be free. She would have needed to love him in the
peace of freedom; for the pursuit of freedom is as much a preoccupation of Kate O'Brien's heroines as the pursuit of love.

The enveloping action, the consolation of Teresa in her illness,
and the hope of securing her peace of mind, comes to a successful
conclusion. The visiting doctors, London and Dublin specialists,
declare against another operation; she is beyond that. But a marriage
between Nurse Cunningham, the day nurse in attendance, and the
ailing Reggie is quietly arranged, and this leaves Teresa free to make
ready her soul and go happily to her death.

There is for the reader here a savage irony, though it lies all in the
juxtaposition of events and in no breathed word. Cunning Nurse
Cunningham and wretched Reggie can arrive at some accommoda-
tion for the future, while the 'god in marble' takes his own life and
the noble girl who loves him is left to make what she can of that

shattering grief. The ante-room, the place of waiting, of suspense, of expectancy has turned out to be a blind-alley. 'This is love — it hardly ever happens', says Vincent to Agnes after they have kissed. 'You mean — it never happens', she answers.

There is little relief in *The Ante-Room* from its taut construction and closed-in texture. What little there is is provided by the ironic treatment of the sexual vanity of Sir Godfrey Barlett-Crowe. Sir Godfrey, the London specialist, considers his journey to the West of Ireland quite an adventure and wonders about the two Irish colleens that he is going to meet — a little masterly coaxing will be in order to put them at their ease, he supposes. The connoisseur of women on all levels 'up and down the social scale' is taken aback to discover that the accomplished and well-bred young ladies of the house are his equals in social ease and that their beauty is not open to any coaxing, no matter how masterly. He retires discomfited from the field.

The Ante-Room was published in 1934, though the setting is the end of the last century: we may take it, I believe, that the moral sensibility with which Agnes Mulqueen is endowed is drawn from the author's moral world, and that Agnes Mulqueen represents the educated Catholic girl of the Irish middle-class from the end of the last century through the opening decades of this. Part of the excitement with which I and my fellow students in U.C.D. greeted the novel on publication was due to the fact that it portrayed an Ireland and a moral dilemma which we recognised as our own.

It is worth noticing, perhaps, that the construction of *The Ante-Room* is exactly like that of a classical play. The three days of the action, All Hallowe'en, All Saints and All Souls, correspond to the three acts of a classical play, and the unities of time, place and action are rigorously observed: even the physical violence, the suicide of Vincent, takes place off-stage, in so far as none of the other characters witness it. The first day may be compared to the exposition of a play, the second leads to the climax, the turning point when Agnes knows and says that she will never go away with Vincent, and the third contains the dénouement or resolution, the effect of which, however, is left to our imagination.

Since the construction is ready-made for a play, it seems surprising that *The Ante-Room*, when it was dramatized, as it was in 1936, failed on the stage, and this in spite of the fact that it was produced by Guthrie McClintick and had as leading lady an actress of some

quality, Diana Wynyard. The tragic ending, however, was altered
and a sort of second-rate happy conclusion supplied — the marriage
of Dr. Curran and Marie-Rose. This runs counter to the whole
thrust of the book, because it is Agnes that Dr. Curran loves and one
of the possibilities open to the reader's imagination at the end is the
future marriage of the two. To substitute Marie-Rose for Agnes is
to change the aura of Agnes's character and to suggest that she is
doomed to spinsterhood: it also alters the impression we have of
Marie-Rose and suggests that she is no more than a predatory
female, ready to appropriate the affections of any available man, at
whatever cost to others. We do not know who was responsible for
this change of direction, whether it was John Perry, who adapted it
for the stage, or McClintick. The feeling of the time was, of course,
against tragedy, as it often is in England: Kate O'Brien herself was
probably bored with the idea of an adaptation; she certainly was
when it came to adapting *That Lady*. It seems that Perry never even
met her, let alone consulted her.

IV

A GIRL AND HER BEAUTY

Mary Lavelle (1936), Kate O'Brien's next novel, is not as well-made as its predecessor: the conflict is not as clipped-in, not as heightened: the heroine is not as decisive, less clearly defined, less intense, dreamier, vaguer: and the device of framing the central action within the illness of an older character is repeated, not so success-fully. But it is a more open investigation of the psycho-sexual development of a girl, Irish and Catholic and Mellick-reared, and it is the first investigation of a girl alone, earning her bread, on the 'errand of keeping alive'.

Mary Lavelle is engaged to be married when she leaves Ireland to spend a year in Spain as a 'Miss'. Her fiancé thinks that they must wait a year before marrying: he hopes by then to be earning more money. Mary wants to get away from her father's peevishness and her aunt Cissy's toadying, and she wants to see something of the world before settling down to becoming a good and dutiful wife. Her fiancé, John, is described as loving her in the usual, straight-forward, bossy, masculine way, she as thinking that she loves him but as not liking to be kissed by him: in other words, her feeling for him is all *agape* and no *eros*. She comes over to the reader as a dutiful, gentle, good girl, but somehow rather dull. But never, it is soon made clear, dull to anyone who looks at her. The point about Mary Lavelle *is* her beauty: she is described as being so beautiful that she makes the old poetic myth of girlhood a reality for every man whose eyes fall on her, even the ailing and elderly Don Pablo, father of her Spanish charges:— 'untouched, unaware, unflirtatious, an unassuming governess-girl . . . unconscious that her brilliant beauty ravished the evening and rendered a sceptical and easily mannered man, her respectable employer, unable to utter more than one or two banal sentences before he hurried away in fear from his own sudden senile folly.' She proves a catalyst for women as well as men: the lonely middle-aged Irish 'Miss', tragic Agatha Conlon, discovers from her confessor that the feeling she has for Mary is wrong — a manifestation of a 'very ancient, terrible vice'.

But it is the love that springs up between the young married son of the house, Juanito, and Mary that lies at the centre of the novel. Neither of them yield easily. Juan is an honest man and he loves his wife: he resents the 'wasteful accident of desire for her'. Mary sees that there is no future for them, both Catholics, both honourable. They must regard the feeling between them as an infatuation which they will have to endure and restrain. She grows up very quickly. On the stolen day at the Hermitage of the Holy Angels, above Toledo, she tells him:—

'I've never been in love, Juanito, until now. So I used to think it is a lovely suitable thing that would grow in its time. I thought I'd like the feeling and be able to manage it and make people happy through it. Just now I don't think it is like that.'

'What do you think?'

'That it is perfectly unreasonable illusion — and must be borne as that. It's of no use. It is not suitable or manageable. It blurs things, puts everything out of focus. It's not a thing to live with. It's a dream.'[1]

From this encounter she takes nothing but a postcard of the Holy Angels, with 'Recuerdo de hoy' written on it by Juan, and a determination to return to Ireland as soon as possible, after a stay of four months, instead of the agreed year. But matters do not rest there. Juan appears suddenly on her last afternoon and drives her up into the Basque countryside above Altorno. There Mary, overcome by her feeling and desolate at the thought of the imminent parting, cannot forbear from kissing him:—

If there was little hope in their kiss and no hint of peace, there was from both all that they possessed of vitality and courage. Moreover, there was love's pure, immense and central delight, which while it did not dim in either brain awareness of past and future, of guilt and responsibility, desolation and shoddy embarrassment, of the meanness of their situation and of the world which made it mean, yet held.[2]

Kissing him, Mary decides that this must not be the end and she asks him to consummate their love. She wants to give all that she has to him. He, fearful for her, does not want to take it, but she insists:— 'Nothing else will content me, however long I live — if you refuse me this.' So, Mary, a young, well-brought up, Irish, Catholic girl, in spite of her training, in spite of the social restraints of her position, in spite of knowing the implications of her behaviour, insists on consummating her love, on experiencing one of life's central mysteries, the giving of one human being to another in love. It is made quite clear that it is the girl who does the choosing.

What follows, we feel, is unnecessary — the death of Don Pablo, also a victim of love for Mary and of jealousy of his son: he had found the postcard with Juan's writing on it which had blown out of Mary's window, had correctly read its implications and, overcome by an attack of angina, had succumbed to illness and emotion. Mary's fatal beauty has been sufficiently emphasised. As a closing movement, the packing of Mary's trunk would have been effective enough, just as the description of its contents in the first chapter makes an effective — and original — opening one. As I have already said, the attempt at making Don Pablo's bad health encompass an enveloping action is not successful in this novel. An opening and a shutting trunk would have done.

Mary had already decided to return to Ireland: the point of the novel had been made — away from family, country and friends, this Irish Catholic girl has reached the same conclusion as Vincent in the earlier novel, that 'there is one thing in the world that is worth regrets and dishonours'. This is the only novel of Kate O'Brien that takes its title from the name of the heroine. Its theme is the growth of this girl from immaturity to womanhood. Seeking a little freedom for a spell, she finds an impossible love, and thereafter all her plans will change, her life will change. She will not now dwindle into a mere wife: she is now a young woman confronting her destiny.

What Kate O'Brien is saying once again through the medium of her art is that for human development love is inescapable and necessary, that it is at once rapture and torture, has nothing to do with happiness: its realisation sometimes a sin, ultimately it is an illusion, yet, she says here, in a passage of authorial intervention:— 'woe to the sunless heart that has never been its dupe.' She is also saying that for girl as much as for man neither the undesigned life nor the pre-arranged is a good thing.

English people may have felt that in writing of the struggles of conscience of Irish girls, Kate O'Brien was, as she once told me an English friend had said, 'a Great Auk writing for other great auks'.

But great auks were not an extinct species in Ireland, and the Censorship of Publications Board took alarm at the audacity of an Irish girl daring to exercise individual judgement, not being led astray — which would be regrettable but pardonable — but choosing to do something which she and they regarded as a grave sin. They banned *Mary Lavelle*, regardless of the fact that by no stretch of the prurient imagination could it be considered 'indecent and obscene', the sole criterion allowed for such action. The Church has always made a place for sinners in its widespread commonwealth, but the Irish state would have none of them. The banning of a book in Ireland was said at the time to be a great boost to its sale abroad, but *Mary Lavelle* was never popular, any more than *The Ante-Room*. *Without My Cloak* remained the author's sole best-seller. Published in 1936, re-printed once, *Mary Lavelle* was issued in the Heinemann pocket edition in 1947: it was also published by Penguin Books.

Kate O'Brien did not like, apart from the damage which it did to her reputation at home, the puritanic and self-righteous phase through which Irish society was going in the thirties — and was to continue to go in the forties — and she wrote two novels which reflected on this society, *Pray for the Wanderer* (1938) after *Mary Lavelle*, and *The Last of Summer* (1943) after *The Land of Spices* (1941), also banned in Ireland; but these are novels with a thesis, written from the intellect only, from the point of view of an onlooker, a visiting brother in the first and a foreign cousin in the second: the author herself appears no more than as a critical commentator, though there is no doubt that both novels were instigated by her own experience of the prevailing temper of the country. I shall have something to say about these novels later on, but to follow the inner development of the novelist, the works 'to which she commits herself', we must turn now to *The Land of Spices*.

V

THE NUN

In *The Land of Spices*, we feel, more than in any other of Kate O'Brien's novels, the projection into her characters of personal anguish. If *Mary Lavelle* showed us a girl saved from the unexamined, undesigned life by an accident of foreign travel, *The Land of Spices* is an examination of a wholly purposeful and dedicated life, though it too was set on its course by an accident, a shock which affected the development of the main character, intervening at a sensitive moment in the growth of an adolescent girl. This character is Mère Marie Hélène Archer, who, when the book opens, is Reverend Mother of an Irish convent of a French Order of nuns, La Compagnie de la Sainte Famille. She entered the convent at the age of eighteen to undertake for the rest of her days the 'impersonal and active service of God', to lead a life every moment of which is to be dedicated to duty or to prayer.

The novel opens with one of those crowded scenes that Kate O'Brien handles so well, the reception of three postulants of the Order in the convent chapel and the Reception Breakfast afterwards. The ceremony is a reminder that the religious life, like the secular, has its own continuity, and the Reverend Mother's thoughts fly back to her own days as a postulant in Bruges and school days in Brussels. The occasion is used to let us know that Reverend Mother is undergoing an attack of dryness of spirit. She is discouraged, not at ease in her present position: she dislikes some manifestations of the Irish temperament, its nationalist aspirations which express themselves in a naïve self-complacency — the novel is set in the opening years of this century — or in arrogant authoritarianism. 'Our nuns are not a nation, and our business is not with national matters', she says to the Bishop. 'We are a religious order'. We are also shown the amusing snobberies and rivalries of the mothers of the postulants, some of the pupils disgracing themselves by an ostentatious attack of *schwärmerei* and the absorbed attention of the new little girl, the baby of the school, six-year old Anna Murphy, as crouched on her hunkers, she watches the ceremony through the bars of her *prie-dieu*.

Folly, snobbery, introspection, inner states of being, the interaction of one human creature on another, the need of the human spirit for love and its equally imperious need to be free, to find a field for the exercise of individual gifts and talents — all these themes cross and interweave through one another in the subsequent development of the novel. It is technically brilliant, intricately and subtly planned; the past, Reverend Mother's past — her family life and religious career — and the present — Reverend Mother's state of soul, the life of the school, family life as found in Anna's family, Anna's life as a schoolgirl — are revealed through flashback scenes and interior monologue, or straightforward description of the present.

Suspense is very well maintained. Not until half through do we learn the reason for Mère Marie Hélène Archer's embracing of the religious life, though in the second chapter, which traces the progress of her religious career, we are told that at eighteen she had been hurled by dynamic shock into the wildest rigours of austerity, 'forever out of reach of all that beauty of human life that she had inordinately believed in — trained most delicately in that belief by the one who was to be its unwitting destroyer'.

That shock had made her afraid of love. Various Reverend Mothers, reporting on her as a young nun, while praising her brilliance as a teacher, her control of her classes, her austerity and devotion, had had to add that she was afraid of love. 'She is afraid of love,' wrote her Reverend Mother when she was in Cracow, 'even of the love of God. This makes me sad for her, for she has very high standards'. Back in Brussels, Mother General has to remind her that 'God is love. And He is served by love'.

The action of the novel reveals Mother Archer's recovery of the ability to forgive her father and to love again, if cautiously and at a distance, another human soul, the child Anna. There are, we might say, two heroines, two characters at the centre of the book, and the Reverend Mother, the mature woman, is as much acted upon by Anna, as Anna is influenced and guided by her. Anna's reciting of a poem, Henry Vaughan's 'My soul, there is a country', at the Sunday ceremony of marksgiving has a crucial influence on the nun. There comes flooding back to her the memory of her own childhood, when she herself had learnt the poem from her father, a specialist in seventeenth-century English poetry. The gravity of the child, the pure thread of the clear little voice soothes Reverend Mother's nerves, restores her courage and confidence in the allotted task which she had been finding so difficult. Back in her study, she tears up the letter she had written to her Mother General, asking to be relieved of her post in Ireland.

By degrees we are taken to the centre of the suffering and struggling spirit of the nun. The news of her father's illness, the receipt of his dying letter, bidding her farewell, leads to a re-living of that brutal incident of her past which had swept her out of the current of ordinary life and into becoming a nun. The young Helen, returning to her home one summer's afternoon to get roses for the convent altar, had come on her father and the young musician, her father's pupil, Etienne, in a homosexual embrace. This revelation, as it was central in her development, comes in the very centre of the novel. The hideous shock, the blind revulsion, anger and jealousy of the young girl, her flight from her father's life, her passionate espousal of the religious life without explanation, her father's bewilderment and hurt, are first laid bare and then the gradual and hard-won recognition by the nun that her father's sins are his own affair, that her arrogance and inability to forgive are sins on her part and merit greater condemnation. At last she reaches the peace of acknowledging that all judgement of sin must be left to God, that for his creature the task is that of fostering in herself only trust in His goodness and tolerance for all her fellow-creatures, that in short, while hating the sin, she must love the sinner.

From the recall of Mother Archer's tragic past, we return to the present, to the conduct of Anna's life and the general life of the school, with all its drama and its moments of exquisite comedy. I cannot readily bring to mind another novel in the English language which so magically and so accurately recreates the life of a convent boarding-school, the exactions of high idealisms and abstractions on the one hand, and on the other the feverishness of adolescents in the grip of developing emotional awareness. On the occasion of Chaplain's concert, the motto of the Order, *La Pudeur et la Politesse*, as practised by the girls, is forced to contain a moment of 'sheer brutal delight in human fatuity'. They listen in agonised self-control to Father Hartigan cracking and banging around on the notes of the difficult 'My dark Rosaleen', and to the young seminarian, his profile 'like a Greek god's', as he finds himself the centre of mysterious feminine flattery when cajoled into singing the wonderfully inappropriate 'Come into the garden, Maud'.

Neither can I recall another novel which recreates so well the spell of convent life, the assaults on the spirit and nerves of the young, the way in which the attraction of renunciation and dedication can combine with a setting of great natural beauty to suggest something beyond natural beauty, beyond anything found on earth, the lure of the Land of Spices. In the following passage we have a typical example of this lyricism:—

On this Sunday evening of May the sky, open and infinite, renewed its glory in the radiant breast of the lake; the hills had the dark bloom of grapes and seemed to breathe and sigh; the impassioned, flaming garden, held in as it was by conventual order and design, seemed for that all the more at breaking point — oblated. The perfume of the wallflowers was palpable, troubling the air. Fuchsia and sweet geranium foamed along the terrace, and pleasure-cries, the distant songs of bathers and boaters, rang sadly to the children from the far shores of the water.

But the trees of the convent spread their wide and tranquillising arms, and the great house stood deep-based in reproachful calm, secure in its rule, secure in Christ against the brief assaults of evening or of roses. Girls about to leave, awaiting life, felt this dismissal by the spirit of the house of the unanswered lovely conflict implicit in the hour; heard the same victory in the voices, beyond the lawn, of nuns taking recreation in Bishop's Walk. And so decided perhaps, tearfully, but in some outlet of feeling, that Mère Marie Félice de Saint Gravons was calling them.[1]

But all such effects must yield to the onward drive of the narrative which flows triumphantly forward to the double climax of Reverend Mother's promotion to the post of Mother-General of the Order and of Anna's winning a County Council scholarship to University College Dublin, which Reverend Mother ensures she can take up against her grandmother's arrogant arrangement of a job in a bank. Reverend Mother's time in Ireland may be seen as a preparation for her call to supreme power in the Order, and Anna, by arousing the suppressed instincts of love in the nun, as helping her. Reverend Mother, before the book opens, has lost the love of her life: Anna, before the book ends, will have lost the love of her life, her brother, Charlie, dead by drowning the previous summer. But Reverend Mother has secured for Anna that liberty for a spell of further education which she has come to regard as the most desirable thing in life and the most difficult for a girl to obtain. She has come to realize that while a boy may expect co-operation in this aim, a girl can do no such thing:— 'she will have to spin it out of herself, as a spider a web.' After defeating Anna's grandmother in the contest about Anna's future, Reverend Mother has the satisfaction of thinking that:— 'Anna was for life now, to make what she could of it.'

Love in *The Land of Spices* is all *agape*. Though expressive of spiritual suffering in many lives, it is ultimately an optimistic book, in that it ends with success for both heroines and in a measure of freedom for both, Reverend Mother freed at last of the obsession with her father's sin and Anna freed of her grandmother's control and able to go on to University. It is also, without a specific word said on the subject, a subtly but profoundly feminist book. The religious life is depicted as offering a career for women, just as it had traditionally offered one to men. There is a ladder of power and influence to be climbed in the hierarchical structure of a great Order of women religious, and Mother Archer is honest enough with herself, when the telegram announcing her appointment as Mother-General arrives, to admit that she likes power:— 'she took pleasure in going as far as it was possible in the life she had chosen.'

The Land of Spices is also feminist in that it shows women as a sisterhood, women supporting and helping one another — the old Mother-General guiding Mother Archer, Mother Archer watching over her flock of nuns and pupils, and especially Anna: in turn the child, Anna, is seen influencing the mature Reverend Mother: even Anna's arrogant old grandmother plays her part by paying Anna's school fees, her father having turned out a drunken failure.

One might go on to claim that the novel hints at further possibilities for women. Towards the end Anna is given a moment of visionary enlightenment that suggests what she had wanted her precious liberty for — the chance of becoming an artist. Attempting to explain *Lycidas* to the pretty, frivolous, South-American girl, Pilar, her attention is deflected from the poem to the girl herself and she suddenly sees her as a motive for art, with 'power to make life compose about it', a 'symbol as complicated as any imaginative struggle in verse; a common piece of creation, an exquisite challenge to creativeness'. Anna feels that this moment was a 'long-awaited, blessed gift'. Anna has received an intimation of what her vocation in life will be. She has been visited by an epiphany. In this we may feel she speaks for the author herself, that in some such moment Kate O'Brien realised what her way in life was to be. We may safely assume that *The Land of Spices* had its origins in some such moment of visionary enlightenment as Anna experienced when she saw the transfigured Pilar as a motive for art.

During the early war years, when Kate O'Brien was working for the Ministry of Information, as well as writing *The Land of Spices*, she first lived in rented rooms in Oxford, then rented a cottage in North Leigh, near Witney, but was in and out of Oxford and up and down from London constantly. It was at this time that she met Enid Starkie, a contemporary who had won her way to higher education and fame by a different route. Though a Catholic, she had gone to Alexandra College for her schooling and had won from there a scholarship in Oxford. Her reputation as a scholar of nineteenth-century French literature was already high when she met her fellow-Irishwoman. She is said to have spoken French more readily than English, and Kate O'Brien mentions in a letter to her sister, Nance, at the time, that she has had Enid Starkie check the French of the letters written in that language in *The Land of Spices*.

The two remarkable Irish women had become friends, but Enid Starkie possessed, among other scholarly gifts, the ruthless honesty that in everyday life can appear naïve, while Kate O'Brien under-stood very well what Dorothy Osborne's brother meant when he said, 'It is a part of good breeding to disguise handsomely.' The friendship languished, therefore, after some time, but Kate O'Brien never lost her admiration for Enid Starkie's relentless application to work nor for the intelligence that set the pursuit of truth above all other aims. But it was an admiration that operated best in absence.

I remember that towards the end of the Roundstone days it was at last possible for Enid Starkie to come on a long-proposed visit of a few days. I was there for the first evening of her stay and, as I listened, I thought how well-matched the pair were in their different styles. In conversation Kate O'Brien flew kites, struck out fancies and made propositions that she did not intend her listeners to take seriously. They were to be caught on the wing, tossed in the air and dropped. Enid Starkie, however, seized on an idea, worried all the meat out of it and only slowly relinquished it. On this occasion she refused to give ground before some sally of Kate's and talked her to a standstill.

The next morning, as I waited for the bus that was to take me as far as Galway, our hostess came into the room, clutching her head and saying, 'My God, I don't know how I am going to endure it. She is sitting up in bed, talking already.' Kate O'Brien had been looking forward to the visit but in the event found Enid Starkie too stimulating. She was worried also about the effect Enid Starkie would have on the village; for she was dressed for her country visit in the costume of a French sailor, complete even to the matelot's cap. The village, as it happened, was well accustomed to eccentricities of apparel and took this, like the rest, in its stride. But Kate O'Brien was afraid that her distinguished visitor might appear a figure of fun, that the fine scholar might seem to the uninitiated like something out of a circus.

After 1942 Kate O'Brien went to live in Cullompton in Devon as a paying guest in the house of another novelist, E. M. Delafield, the author of the best-selling *Diary of an English Country Lady*. It was while she was living there she wrote *The Last of Summer* (1943). This friendship was cut short by the untimely death of E. M. Delafield.

VI

THE GREAT LADY

It so happens that we do know the occasion when Kate O'Brien was visited by the epiphany which led to her novel *That Lady* (1946). In an article in *University Review* which had been previously delivered as a lecture to the N.U.I. Graduates Association on 2 May 1963, she writes:—

One very bad wet night in January 1940 I was working hard in my flat in Bloomsbury — and I went out in the rain in the blackout to the letter-box at the corner. I imagine that I was in a dull and non-receptive mood — and certainly nothing was further from my upper brain than thoughts of Spain and Spanish history. But suddenly, just as I was putting the letters through the slot, I was invaded by what seemed to be an *entire* novel which I was one day to write and which was to be called *That Lady*. I remember being as if dazzled in a flash. I leant against the letter-box in the rain, still clutching the letters in the slot, taking in the whole conception. The woman, the Princess of Eboli, had been visiting and re-visiting me for years as interesting but not my cup of tea. All of a sudden she and her history took clear possession of me — by that letter-box in the rain. I suppose I saw and, as it were, wrote the whole book. And I felt superbly happy . . .
Yet I did not begin to write *That Lady* until five years later in 1945. That night I knew it was a settled thing — and in view of all the labour, all the worry, all the despair and doubts, I can't help smiling at my innocent self-satisfaction that night.[1]

We know that it was in the letters of St. Teresa of Avila that Kate O'Brien first came across mention of the Princess of Eboli, because she told us so herself in a talk on Radio Telefís Éireann, called 'Self-Portrait', first televised in 1962 and repeated on 5 February 1983. She also said on that occasion that she always wrote from 'reflection on people'.

This — the writing of *That Lady* — was the first time that the people she reflected on were characters established in history and not obscure members of the rising Irish bourgeoisie, or people living in Ireland. In a brief foreword, she writes:— 'what follows is not a historical novel. It is an invention arising from reflection on the curious external story of Ana de Mendoza and Philip II of Spain.' What the historian failed to explain she attempts. She attempts to understand the actions of Ana de Mendoza and Philip II through the dictates and impulses of their inner life, the promptings of will and passion, the principles that guide behaviour.

The heroine here is a great lady of Spain, daughter of the Mendozas, an heiress, who had been married to Ruy Gomez, favourite Minister of State of Philip II, at the latter's instigation. Ana from childhood has liked and admired Philip: she had once thought that she was destined to be his bride: he has indulged himself by thinking that only his virtue and his friendship for Gomez has prevented him from making her his mistress. When the novel opens, she is a widow of thirty-six, with six surviving children, and has been requested by Philip to return from her country estate of Pastrana to Madrid. Seeing her hesitation, he asks:— 'Shall I perhaps have to command you, Ana?' And she thinks:— 'Was he then becoming a blind autocrat? Did he truly think he could *command* a subject in a private matter?' But that, precisely, is what the jealous, autocratic, dog-in-the-manger King does think, and that is the pivot on which the novel hinges.

Ana, the greatest lady in Spain, a Castilian with centuries of noble ancestry behind her, is depicted as having immense self-confidence, and as regarding Philip as something in the nature of a *parvenu* in her country. She likes to indulge him with a show of reverence and never fails in offering the usual public courtesies, but she feels free to speak her mind and is capable of reminding the king that neither he, nor her late husband, knew anything of the Castilian nobility from the inside, nor could speak for them as she could. Now, to her astonishment, she discovers that she is expected, because of her widowhood, to regard herself as a ward of the King, not free to dispose of herself.

Ironically, the King's insistence on Ana's return to Madrid brings back into her life Antonio Perez, once a pupil of Ruy Gomez, and now in succession to him, chief Minister of State. In a short time Ana and Perez become lovers, and the King, through the intrusion into Ana's life of another survivor from the past, the mad, puritanic

Juan de Escovedo, also a Minister of State, gets to know of the erotic involvement of Ana, to whom the King never afterwards refers except as 'Essa Senora', that lady. Ana, who, like an earlier heroine, Agnes Mulqueen, is Catholic to the backbone and who has never regarded her love for Perez, a married man, with many children, as anything but a sin, and has begun to feel that she must repent and put Perez out of her life, is now driven back on her Castilian sense of honour, thinking that her concern for her conscience must yield to her loyalty for a fellow-human being. For Juan de Escovedo had outrageously broken in on the Princess of Eboli's privacy one night when Perez was with her; but his treacherous plans for Don John of Austria having been discovered by Philip, the King, typically pursuing a crafty, Machiavellian plot, has given orders to Perez to have Escovedo assassinated. He thus exposes Perez to the suspicions of the people, who think Perez has done away with Escovedo for his own reasons, and refuses to have a public trial held. Both Ana and Perez know that Perez is now in deadly danger from the King. She coolly defies the King's presumption that his rights as a sovereign include the right to dictate the behaviour of a free citizen of Castile in private matters, and continues to give Perez open support.

What Ana does not understand is that to the King's tortuous, vain and devious way of thinking there is no distinction between private and political life. He has become a despotic ruler, and Ana shows herself politically naïve in imagining that such rulers confine themselves to despotism in the public sphere. All power, all permissions emanate from them. Ana has not realised the truth expressed centuries afterwards in the famous dictum of Lord Acton:— 'All power tends to corrupt: absolute power tends to corrupt absolutely.' Inevitably her fight for freedom in private life takes on a political colouring, and she is encouraged to believe, by those whose opinion she respects, like the Cardinal Archbishop of Toledo, that her stand is not only justifiable but laudable. As she says to the Marques de Los Velos, 'One doesn't submit private lives to public tests.'

But Philip thinks of Ana as a piece of property. He had 'given' her to Ruy Gomez. What he has given he is free to withhold. His possessiveness is outraged by her taking a lover and by what he considers her insolence to him. He strikes at her physical freedom, his anger and jealousy finding ever more brutal expression. She is first carried off by night from her Madrid house and incarcerated in a common prison, an isolated keep some miles distant from the capital, next sent home to her country estate at Pastrana and held as a house prisoner, the arrangement of her estates taken from her, her quarters confined to a few rooms from which the valuables have been stripped, and finally, because she has received a visit from Antonio in flight to Aragon, bricked up in a single room, kept in darkness and misery, her health failing, her faithful duenna banished, her only comfort the presence of her youngest child, Anichu, who has refused to be parted from her. She dies undefeated, a martyr, one might say, to the principle of the individual citizen's right to order his private life in freedom.

That Lady is clearly based on an intellectual idea. The material used to embody the idea is taken from history, and the main characters are historical figures, but their motives for action, the understanding of their behaviour, come from the spirit of the writer herself and the world she lived in. A flaw in the novel, *qua* novel, is the failure to make convincing the love between Ana and Perez. Ana is depicted as first coldly indulging in that exercise called 'taking a lover': she is then supposed to have developed a true love for Antonio. But in this novel the writer's interest is not centred on love; it is on freedom. And what is convincing is Philip's horrible love-hatred, his jealous possessiveness and power to give rein to his ignoble feelings, and Ana's independence of spirit, her calm repudiation of his right to that possessiveness, and later her equally calm — and eventually heroic — defiance of his despotic behaviour.

That Lady was written in 1945. As we have seen, it was conceived in 1940. We cannot but feel that the state of Europe at the time, the Nazi despotism and brutality, is reflected in the brutal despotism of Philip II, and that Ana may be seen as a prototype of the political martyrs of those war years. She is a woman who claims the right to freedom in the conduct of private life and the right to open trial in civil and criminal charges. She is refused both rights by a man who happens to have political power over her, a 'half-foreign King'. Vast areas of Europe were refused the same rights by the mad little Austrian house-painter, Adolf Hitler, against whom England stood alone during the early part of the Second World War.

Ana is sustained by other women in her struggle against the King, first by her faithful duenna, Bernardina, who again and again defies the King's orders to leave the Princess, and afterwards, when Bernardina has been finally banished, by her youngest child,

Anichu, who shares her last privations. The consolations of *agape*, therefore, remain hers, but her right to erotic fulfilment has been savagely denied. The story of the Princess of Eboli demonstrates that social position and great wealth do not guarantee a woman personal freedom, and that for a sensitively intelligent woman, no matter in what position and no matter where, the freedom to love is as hard to come by as the opportunity to love in freedom.

In the novels so far treated we see that the cost of loving for a woman can be no less than the loss of the direction of her life by herself, the loss of her worldly goods, the loss of happiness, the loss of life itself. This is true of the novels set in Ireland during or at the end of the last century and the beginning of this, as it is of novels set in the Spain of the sixteenth century, which stands as a paradigm of the middle years of this century when Nazi despotism blackened the skies of Europe and kindled the fires of political martyrs. Kate O'Brien's novels are a chronicle of her time as much as anything.

VII

ASIDES

The four novels already discussed represent the best work of Kate O'Brien, and since they have a common theme, in different settings, the pursuit of love and freedom by intelligent woman, I have grouped them together. We must now turn to the two novels that I call 'asides', *Pray for the Wanderer* (1938) and *The Last of Summer* (1943): they were both written in response to the banning of a previous book, after *Mary Lavelle* and *The Land of Spices* respectively. Kate O'Brien could well feel aggrieved by the banning of these books, especially by that of *The Land of Spices*. The criterion, as I have already said, supposed to guide the Censorship Board was that of a book 'being in general tendency indecent and obscene'; the objection, it emerged, to *The Land of Spices* was to a single sentence, to the sentence where Helen Archer finds her father and Etienne 'in the embrace of love'. Either members of the Censorship Board were clearly not keeping their own rules, or Church and State at the time identified virtue with ignorance. The Chairman, Professor Magennis, also a Senator, waxed magnificently eloquent in expression of his horror and disgust at any reference to such a subject and his fear for the young people of the country, if they were to learn of its existence. Today, when every formerly taboo subject is discussed on radio and television, it is difficult to understand all the furore. At the time sensible and fair-minded people protested against the banning, pointing out that the principles of justice were contravened when a book could be banned for a single sentence and the author thereof judged to have produced a work in general tendency indecent and obscene. Protests failed: the book was banned, not, of course before those really interested had read it.

Apart from the damage to her own reputation which the vagaries of the new Calvinism in Irish society caused, Kate O'Brien did not like the illiberal, self-complacent and Puritanic society that developed in Ireland in the thirties and forties of this century. She

75

saw de Valera as a milder, more skilful variant of the dictators that
had come to power in so many countries in Europe. *Pray for the
Wanderer* has only the flimsiest of plots, a few loose pegs on which
a discussion of Ireland's condition is hung. The author herself is
present, no longer in the guise of an aspiring young woman or a
suffering older one, but as a man, a famous author back in Ireland
on a visit to his brother and sister-in-law. The flimsy plot turns on
the fact that the famous man, Matt Costello, is seeking asylum
from a love that has ended unhappily, that he is attracted to the cool
beauty of Nell Mahoney, his brother's sister-in-law, and imagines
temporarily that he will reform, return to Ireland and, married to
Nell, live an examplary life like his brother. Nell is too intelligent
not to discern the emotional state of Matt: she has no intention of
being any man's cure, and besides, has her own allegiances to the
past. The book ends with Matt deciding to return to England. But
this sketchy background serves merely as an excuse for what is in
reality a tract for the times. In long discussions between Matt and
Tom Mahoney, cousin of Nell and old college friend of Matt, and
between Matt, Tom and Father Malachi, Tom's Franciscan friend,
the present state of Ireland is dissected, the nature of the artist's work
and his contribution to society is considered and the Irish psyche
declared to be essentially moralistic, not artistic. Tom Mahoney,
cynical and mocking, is used from within Irish society to jibe at the
hypocrisy and religiosity of the times:-

Religiosity is becoming a job in this country, you might say. A plank. A
threat and a menace. A power in the land, in fact, my boy! In the Island of
Saints and Scholars! Yah — it's disgusting! It's a matter of municipal policy
now wearing this little button and that little badge, holding a banner here
and running to make a retreat there, with Father O'Hegarty warning you
kindly about this, and Father O'Hartigan rapping you over the knuckles
about that and Father O'Hanigan running off to the bishop to talk about
you! Town Council stuff! Pure jobbery. 'But is he a good practising
Catholic, Father O'Dea?' 'And are you sure he leads a moral life, Sister
Mary Joseph?' And if you aren't sure, will you kindly make it your life-
work to find out! My God, it's terrible! We need an Ibsen here, Matt.[1]

Even Nell Mahoney is affected by her environment. She thinks
everyone should toe the line, nobody claim privilege: she dis-
approves of the expression of individuality, believes in the ordering
of society so as to produce the greatest happiness of the greatest

number, is, in short, an authoritarian. If we remember the previous novels, this must appear ironic. For Nell Mahoney has attained to one of the goals of the O'Brien heroines, personal and economic freedom. She has been educated to university level and is well equipped to earn her own living: she can travel in her free time, and dresses well: she does not seem to need the protection of either marriage or the convent. But Nell was once engaged to be married to the free-thinking Tom, her cousin; she had become estranged from him when she discovered an incident in his past life, a brief *amour* with a shop-girl which had resulted in an illegitimate child. It gradually becomes clear that, proud and obstinate though they both are, they will come together again, that the jealousy which Matt's attentions to Nell stir up in Tom will melt the ice between them.

Matt's brother, Will, is depicted as a sensitively loving man, happily married to a generous wife who already has five children and is expecting a sixth. They are well-off, contented, civilised people who do not approve of many things taken for granted by those around them — the corporal punishment of children at school, for instance — but are certainly not going to take a stand on such matters. Because his wife's arms are always open to him, Will is happy: with a less accessible wife, one not prepared to take the consequences of accepting at all time the demands of a loving husband, his happiness would have been wrecked. The point is not stressed: it is there for the reader to take. This wife is not a victim, but in a society organized on such lines many a wife might be. The point *is* made, however, that in other circumstances, Una, the wife, would not have been a strong character, but probably a complainer and a whiner. Will and Una are happy, in short, not because they accept the ethos of their time, but because, by chance, they are compatible and their marriage is a refuge for both.

Matt is at variance with all this. Using Nell to comment on him, the author has her think:-

His face . . . revealed even more than his books that he was one who must pursue life and control it through personal feeling. It was probable that only by deep and perhaps cruel or selfish knowledge of one or two fellow-creatures he had come to his present quite adequate novelist's equipment of general understanding. Emotion had brought him to observation, but emotion came first and would always be his sheet anchor, for better or

worse . . .. The only way to know him would be to quicken to him in
response to his own unpredictable quickening. Then, as open as a daisy
while the mood held, he would give you all there was of Matt Costello,
and welcome. But you must move him first. That was the *sine qua non*.[2]

Here we have one character within the novel commenting on
another, but that other is a *persona* for the author; so, in effect, what
we have is disguised autobiography, the author in the disguise of a
male character making a case for individual judgement and the life
of the feelings. This does not result in a good novel, but *Pray for the
Wanderer* is interesting as a documentary on the confessional Ireland
of the time and valuable as a record of the author's thinking on the
subject, in response to the way in which she, as a creative writer,
had been treated by the state.

The title is taken from a hymn sung commonly at May devotions
in Catholic churches. It is redolent of nostalgia, but we must also,
given the attitude of Matt Costello, see it as ironic. Matt is a
wanderer, but can he in truth call on the Queen of Heaven to pray
for him?

> Hail, Queen of Heaven, the Ocean Star,
>   Guide of the wand'rer here below;
> Thrown on life's surge, we claim thy care;
>   Save us from peril and from woe.
> Mother of Christ, Star of the sea,
>   Pray for the wand'rer, pray for me.

I loved this hymn when I was a child, not for devotional reasons, I
am afraid, but because I liked the imagery of the Ocean Star and the
tossed human beings on the waves below. A final irony in its use
here must reside in its composition by an Englishman, Father
Faber.

As usual, the natural background to the lives of the characters,
Matt Costello's native Mellick and surrounds, is filled in with a
delicate appreciation of its subtle contrasts. On an expedition westward from the city, Matt looks backward on the view he had
desired to see:-

Mellick lay at the heart of it, in the green watered valley. A gravely poised
city, old and quiet; the river swung beside it and outward south and west
in brilliant loops and unfurlings towards the sea. The Vale of Honey spread

east in summer richness to Tipperary's mountains, blue but even now snow-touched upon the peaks. Westward, in the foreground, the green and granite country, already expectant of the sea, shelved up in desolation.[3]

That summer richness and that granite desolation have produced Matt Costello. But it is not enough to hold him.

As we have seen, *Pray for the Wanderer* represents a time of stock-taking for the author and of comment on Irish society. The same is true of *The Last of Summer*, written after the banning of *The Land of Spices*. It is a better novel than *Pray for the Wanderer*, and its repudiation of the values of the self-protective, self-satisfied Ireland that confronts the outbreak of the second World War with the armour of amused neutrality all the stronger because not expressed so directly. The device of the outsider is used again to throw into relief an established system of values, but this time the outsider is not a mature man temporarily licking his wounds, but a vulnerable young girl, a French cousin who, touring Ireland with some actor friends and finding herself near her unknown Irish cousins, decides on an impulse to visit them. The evolution of the plot is bound up with the imminent approach of war in late summer, 1939, and this suspense from without adds to the internal suspense created in the Kernahan household by the advent of Angéle.

The triumph of the novel is not the story of the love that springs up between Angéle and her cousin, Tom, but the character of Mrs Kernahan, Angéle's Aunt-in-law, Aunt Hannah. She is a woman of formidable self-possession and complacency, armed with insular indifference to everybody and everything outside her immediate circle and her immediate interests: a figure of Pharasaical self-deception, she uses her piety as a cover for her selfishness, and gently tramples on anyone who dares to resist her will. The apple of her eye is her elder son, Tom, whom she loves with passionate possessiveness and rules with the iron hand in the velvet glove.

Into her drawing-room wanders the innocent, trusting Angéle. She creates havoc in the household. It turns out that Aunt Hannah had never told her children of Angéle's existence: her father, Aunt Hannah's brother-in-law, by leaving Ireland, going to live in Paris and marrying a French actress had, it seems, put himself beyond the pale. Angéle's cousins, the two young men, Tom and Martin, and their sister, Jo, are delighted with Angéle. Both Tom and Martin fall in love with her: she falls in love with Tom and accepts his proposal of marriage. But before the necessary dispensation can be arranged, war is declared. Angéle must return to France, and Tom is persuaded by his mother of his selfishness in thinking of taking Angéle away from her own way of life and burying her in the country. Martin, she points out, is much more Angéle's type. Tom bows to his mother's judgement and Angéle leaves even more unceremoniously than she arrived. We hear that Martin too intends returning to France, where he hopes, in spite of war, to continue with his travelling studentship. So, possibly, we are left feeling, Angéle and Martin may continue their acquaintanceship in France.

But the plot is not what is significant here: the skill of the writer is devoted to the creation of Hannah Kernahan's character and the emotional stranglehold which she has on her elder son, whose love is a compensation for, indeed an improvement on, the love of her dead husband. Hannah Kernahan, by the exercise of sheer will-power, in the service of vanity, has made her world exactly what she wants it to be. In the course of the novel we learn that her contempt for Angéle's father is based, not on the fact that she jilted him, as the official version has it, but that he jilted her. Injured pride has prevented all reference to him, his French wife or his daughter. Like many an Irish mother of the time, she has found consolation in the love of her son for any deficiencies of feeling between her second-best choice of husband and herself. She has found for herself, in a dependent relation, Dotey, a dim-witted, greedy but toadying housekeeper. This leaves her free to embroider vestments for her church and take comforting strolls in the garden with Tom. She is oblivious to the need for Tom to prove his manhood and find a companion for himself. The approach of war leaves her untouched. What has a European war got to do with Ireland, she asks, whenever the matter is raised. She infuriates Martin, and Jo is about to escape her by entering a convent. But Tom is held captive. Angéle has never the ghost of a chance against her. Norrie O'Dowd, the sturdy daughter of the local doctor, may be allowed to marry Tom in Hannah's own good time.

This study of frustration finding compensation in power is new to Kate O'Brien's work. In Hannah she gives us her only extensively studied character of a mother, and a mother's relations with her children. It is, perhaps, significant that the telling relationship is that between the mother and her elder son. Kate O'Brien did not remember her own mother, except, as she described it, in 'sweet flashes.' She creates no loving sustained relationship between a mother and daughter, except that between the sixteenth-century Ana de Medoza and Anichu. In this novel, the only girl, Jo, regards her mother with anxious detachment, making half-excuses to Angéle for her behaviour. She would never dream of seeking sympathy from her mother, or of confiding in her. Martin, while he sees through her, can yet yield to his mother's charm and the apparent calm with which she confronts all problems.

New too is another feature of the novel. We have a gallery of grotesques, Dotey, Maggie May, the barmaid in Mrs Cusack's pub, Mrs Cusack herself, Bernard, the crazed, unfrocked priest, who lives in the background of the Kernahan household with his brother, the groom, and his sister-in-law; even Uncle Corney, another semi-dependent of the house, may be included. All these are abnormal, leading not fully realised or blighted lives.

Altogether, what we get here is a very unattractive picture of Ireland in the late thirties, where the powerful people are smug, vain and narrow-minded, and the gentle are weak and pathetic victims, where, as in a Ben Jonson play, we can take our choice between folly and wickedness. Angéle is not sufficiently strong to act as counter-weight to all this native cunning and selfishness: she too falls into the category of victim. There is no direct authorial comment, and Martin and Jo, the only native characters intelligent and sympathetic enough to know or care what terrible evil is gathering its forces to loose on the world, are too young and carry too little authority to balance their elders.

But if the people are disappointing, the countryside is as beautiful and seductive as ever, with the same magical gleam, the same play of light and water, the same ever-changing skies. One of the scenes that stays in the mind is the day spent at the sea-side by all the young people. This is the kind of day that Kate O'Brien herself loved, a day of harmless, innocent, outdoor amusement. I have seen her at the Connemara Pony Show spend hours of absorbed happiness, listening to the remarks of the country people and watching with an eye inherited from her father the lovely Connemara ponies. The place in the novel is not Connemara, of course, but Lahinch, a sea-side resort surpassed in her experience only by Kilkee and serving here to provide a day of pleasure, in contrast to the grim struggle in the Kernahan household and the grimmer one hovering on the horizon.

Kate O'Brien herself spent the war in England, working for the Ministry of Information and writing a novel that appeared on the surface to have nothing to do with the 1939–1945 war. But, as I have already pointed out, *That Lady* turns on the theme of freedom of the individual *versus* the tyranny of the despotic ruler, though individual and ruler are set back in the sixteenth century. One might have expected her to have continued her exploration of woman's need for both love and freedom into the period contemporary with her own life, instead of removing it to history. One can only guess at the reasons. A failure of nerve? A realization that if *The Land of Spices* were banned, such a novel would have been given to the flames in her native country? A fear of offending her family, to whose feelings she remained most delicately responsive all her life? An inability to write well too near her subject? Whatever the reasons, she said what she had to say through the medium of the past.

VIII

TWO GIRLS IN SEARCH OF AN EDUCATION

In November 1946 Kate O'Brien was invited as guest of honour to the Annual Dinner of the Women Writers Club in Dublin. The intention was to celebrate *That Lady* which had had an immense success and become a best-seller. Micheál MacLiammóir was asked to propose the toast to our guest and I to second it. With her usual graciousness she came up to me afterwards and congratulated me on my speech, as if I, and not she, were the celebrity of the evening. She told me that I was one of the three best public speakers she had ever heard! Overcome by such praise, I hastily turned the conversation back to her and told her with what eager admiration I and my fellow-students had read *Without My Cloak* and *The Ante-Room* when they first appeared. A few days afterwards she invited me to lunch, and so began a memorable and stormy friendship.

At the time she was staying in the Shelbourne Hotel, enjoying the success of her latest novel and spending the money she was making from its sale like wildfire. Though no business woman myself, I thought this reckless and I suggested to her that she should invest some of her money while she still had any. The only way of investing money that I knew anything about was buying a house, so I advised her to buy a house, in Ireland, of course, since she seemed to want to live in Ireland. I also, I remember, suggested Connemara, thinking it a suitably romantic place for a romantic novelist. It was years before I realized I had given her the wrong advice. She was no Wordsworthian and needed the cut and thrust of sophisticated human society much more than she needed a romantic place to live in. Perhaps at the time she herself did not fully realize this; for she seemed to think my idea a good one.

It was, however, some years before she could attempt to put the idea into practice. For one think she was invited by Guthrie McClintick to dramatize *That Lady* for the North American stage, with his wife, the great actress Katherine Cornell, in the title role. She worked on this on and off for a couple of years and then in autumn of 1949 sailed for the United States. The play was tried out on tour before being put on on Broadway. It was reasonably successful, but being reasonably successful is not the same thing as a runaway success, and Kate O'Brien did not make the kind of money that she had expected to and that would have compensated her for the time spent on the work. I think that already when she set about dramatizing *That Lady* she was bored with the subject and wanted to get on with the next novel. I saw the play when it was put on in Dublin and thought it was too discursive and failed to reach a dramatic climax: the material probably needed much more drastic re-shaping than it had been given.

By 1950 Kate O'Brien was back in Dublin and set about exploring Connemara for a place to live in; after the usual wild-goose chases, she found a house that would serve, the former residence of the dispensary doctor, in Roundstone, a charming village on the coast, about ten miles from Clifden. She described it rather contemptuously as a Victorian villa, and it certainly was in a dilapidated state. But it had possibilities and with some additions and improvements could be made into a roomy and attractive dwelling. Called The Fort, it was built on its own little promontory, looking south-eastwards across the bay to the Twelve Pins, a view that was never less than impressive and at times took on an unearthly beauty, became a vision of Hy-Brasil, with the purple-blue mountains and the rosy-purple sea stained by the setting sun.

She bought it and set about the necessary restorations and improvements. The people of the village welcomed her arrival: it was a feather in their cap to have a famous author choose to live among them. She for her part delighted in the easy conviviality of the place, and not a day passed but she strolled up to the village to visit post-office and pub, butcher and grocer. But gradually it became clear that there were drawbacks to living in so remote a spot. Her friends could visit her, but in the nature of things they could not stay for long: in the summer she became a sort of show-piece, and strangers, on the flimsiest of excuses, claiming to have been at school with her youngest brother, or to have a copy of a novel that they would like autographed, pushed open her garden gate and knocked on her door. There was no question of her not being at home: she could be seen in her study. I remember telling her that, if I were she, I should lock the front gate and go in and out by the back entrance. But no: she continued to sit, the observed of all observers, and have her time taken and her work interrupted by all comers at all hours. I never understood this; for Kate O'Brien could manifest, when she chose, a withering boredom. She would object strenuously on such occasions as she found herself beside what she called a 'repetitious old bundle', or a 'self-complacent tulip of a woman', or a 'vain ass of a man'. But old bundles, complacent tulips and vain asses were allowed to invade her study on the pretext of having read this novel or the other, or having met her sister in Grafton Street, or of having gone to school to the Crescent in Limerick when her brother was there.

There were other perils in her situation. Delighting in the ever-changing beauty of the countryside, as she did, she had bought a second-hand baby Fiat in order to get around. But she had no affinity with machines of any kind: she was the kind of driver who seems to grind her way through the gears by sheer will-power. The roads at the time were bad in Connemara, very twisty and sandy-surfaced. Once, driving by Ballinafad, she misjudged the second curve on the road and, instead of continuing on the road, jumped the bridge and landed on the ground below. Normally there would have been water there, but it happened to be the one dry fortnight of the summer. A lorry-driver coming from the opposite direction was petrified by what he saw and thunderstruck when the driver emerged unscathed from the car. I asked her what she had felt when she found herself sailing over the bridge. 'I remembered', she said, 'the advice of my father. He always said "if your horse is inclined to bolt with you, throw your weight back in the saddle." So I threw myself back in the saddle and, as you have heard, landed on all fours.'

Between sightseeing and sight-seers, there was not much time left during the day for working: this she did mainly at night and by 1952 had finished another novel, *The Flower of May*: it was published in 1953. The strategy — if strategy it was — of taking her material from the past had worked with *That Lady*, in the sense that there had been no banning of that book, though sins of the flesh are committed and independence of judgement exercised in it as freely as in the banned pair. In *The Flower of May* she reverts in time to the beginning of the century and re-introduces the Belgian convent of Mother Archer and the old Mother General who had watched over

Mother Archer, but the setting is different. No longer is it Mellick, but Dublin and Clare, with excursions to Belgium and Italy.

The theme is the old one, of the pursuit of love and freedom, and specifically here of education as a means of self-fulfilment and independence. There are two heroines, the Irish girl, Fanny, and the Belgian, Lucille. They met at the Belgian school, which both attend, and had become friends when each discovered the other to be the most intelligent of her schoolfellows.

Fanny has been sent to school at Place des Ormes in Brussels, because her mother and her aunt, Delahunts, belonging to the minor landed gentry, we are told, have been at school there before her. Fanny, we find, as the story opens, has been shocked to discover that because of the marriage of her elder sister, Lilian, her parents will not allow her to finish her final year and sit her *Bachot* examination, but, instead, expect her to stay at home and be a comfort to them, until she, in turn, marries. This, insisted on by her gentle, dreamy mother as well as her sentimental father, is accepted by everybody as the proper and normal thing. Fanny, disappointed, tries to argue her case and then sadly resigns herself to not going back to school. For a while she hopes that she may be allowed to return for a short time before the examination and cram for it. Even this is denied her. What use would the *Bachot* be to her? She will marry in due course, like her sister. This attitude is not surprising for the period, considering even so few French girls then attempted the examination. Fanny is determined on one thing — not to be married off to the first eligible young man who presents himself.

Fanny then is one of those who do not intend to lead the unexamined, undesigned life, but *The Flower of May* is a sentimental rehearsal of a theme that has been more strongly rendered before: it evolves into a Cinderella-type story, with all Fanny's difficulties dissolved away, her mother dying at fifty; her father's sister, Aunt Edith, wishing to take up residence with her brother; André-Marie de Saint Mellin, Lucille's brother, who had a little troubled Fanny's serenity, being exposed as a cold-blooded seducer; and last and best of all, her Aunt Eleanor deciding to leave the Delahunt family house and farm to Fanny and to give her an allowance on the security of the property, which will allow her to pursue her education at the Sorbonne, or wherever she chooses. Aunt Eleanor even suggests that, if Lucille fails in her struggle with her wealthy father to get time and money for her education, she could borrow a further £100 per year on Glassala House and she and Fanny could manage on the combined income.

It seems to me that there is a certain muffling of the possibilities in Fanny's character. She is presented as at once gentle and firm, sympathetic to others but tenacious of her own purposes: physically she has a strong resemblance to her frail, absent-minded mother, but temperamentally is quite different: she has no intention of playing a passive role in life, supporting the sensibilities of someone like her foolish, sentimental father. It is as if Kate O'Brien were observing her heroine from without and not unravelling her from the springs of her own being. It is a pity that Fanny's difficulties are all solved for her and her inner strength not tested; for at the end of the novel, when she out-faces André de Saint Mellin and forces him to agree to return to France and leave her sister, Lilian, alone, she shows that she has the nerve and resolution to gain her ends.

The novel begins well, with one of those set pieces that the novelist handles brilliantly, the wedding of Lilian Morrow to Michael, a member of the up-and-coming O'Connors. But the machinery of the plot creaks. André-Marie de Saint Mellin's arrival with his Mercedes, the sale of which he is promoting in Ireland, just as the wedding party is beginning to break up, the seduction of Lilian on her very honeymoon, the unexpected death of Julia — all seem forced, strained, implausible. Certain things that are emphasised seem irrelevant, or unexploited, such as Cousin Bill's drunken cynicism, for instance, or the beam of the lighthouse in Glassala that is never curtained off.

There are, however, several new things attempted in *The Flower of May*. One is the mother-daughter relationship, which is twice portrayed here, that of Fanny and her mother and of Lucille and her mother. Julia shows the same dreamy selfishness to Fanny as she had done to her sister, Eleanor, sacrificing everybody to her husband: one might say that her death will prove a convenience for Fanny. Lucille is a much stronger characrter than her mother: here the roles are reversed, the charming, silly Countess proving wax in the hands of he strong-minded daughter. Neither relationship is very convincing, Kate O'Brien's lack of personal experience perhaps showing here. Neither mother is sympathetic to her daughter's real needs.

Another new relationship depicted in the novel is that between Fanny and Lucille, unlikely though such a friendship may seem between the wealthy, assured Lucille and the not so well-off, withdrawn Fanny. To begin with, evidence of intelligence attracts each to the other, but this attraction has strengthened into a true emotional bond, an *amitié amoureuse*, in which Lucille has as much to gain as she has to give. The delineation of really vicious people here is also new in Kate O'Brien's work, coldly sensual people. One such is Lilian, Fanny's sister, and another is André-Marie, Lucille's brother.

Finally there is the introduction of a comic character, the maid Honoria, who is almost a stage Irishwoman, and fulfils no real function either in the plot or the characterisation. The comic relief she provides is at one stage irrelevant and later inappropriate.

We may notice that here, as in *The Land of Spices* and in *That Lady*, it is the women who help other women. It is Fanny's Aunt Eleanor who makes it possible for Fanny to realize her wishes. Eleanor had had her own intentions in life frustrated: she had wished to become a nun, but when Julia married and removed to Dublin, she had had to stay and look after her father and the estate. We may also notice that mothers are as little use to their daughters as fathers are: they want them to follow the set, conventional lines. The direct family bond here is restrictive. Help has to come from a concerned but also a detached source.

The Flower of May is a book of considerable charm, but of nostalgic charm. It does not take the writer into new fields: it plays variations on old tunes: and some of the variations die on the air without making the point of their introduction clear.

IX

TWO STUDENT-SINGERS IN SEARCH
OF A CAREER

The Flower of May was published in 1953. Kate O'Brien spent the
early months of 1954 in Italy, in preparation for her next novel,
which was to be called *As Music and Splendour* (1958). I was on
sabbatical leave in Rome from 1953 to 1954, so I know something at
first-hand of the research that went into the writing of the
background of the novel. She lived in Rome in the historic centre of
the city, *il centro*, and when she writes about Via di Greci, Piazza del
Popolo, Trastevere, or the acacia trees on the Pincio, she is writing
about places that had not changed much since the time depicted in
the novel. She travelled to Naples, Milan and Ferrara to see the opera
houses in these cities and listen to the singing they provided. In
Milan she heard Maria Callas singing in the *répétition générale* of
Gluck's *Orphée et Eurydice* and in Verdi's *Don Carlos*. It was a great
privilege to be admitted to a *répétition générale* at *La Scala*, and I think
that Maria Callas's absolute control of voice and gesture contributed
to the description of Rose's singing when she has her triumph in La
Scala. In addition to listening to the singers of her day, Kate O'Brien
read up the history of opera, of opera houses, and the professional
training of singers. All this background material is scrupulously
accurate.

But Kate O'Brien had an advantage other than accuracy of preparation in writing a novel about Irish singers and Italian opera. She
had a life-long interest in music and had herself the gift of perfect
pitch. When she was a child, one of the greatest treats of the family
was to be taken during the Christmas holidays to Cork to hear the
D'Oyly Carte Opera Company perform in the Opera House of
that city. Her sister Clare had a voice of such quality that, had she
chosen, she could have made a career of singing. Moreover, it so
happened that Marguerite Burke-Sheridan, the Irish soprano who
had had such a success as Madame Butterfly in Puccini's opera as is

ascribed to Rose as Desdemona in the novel, had returned to Ireland in the mid-fifties and was living in Dublin. As a schoolgirl in Dominican College, Eccles Street, I had caught glimpses of the great Burke-Sheridan when she came to visit her old school and Mother Clement, her first singing mistress, who had set her on the road to success. She must have been at the height of her career then and she seemed like a bird of Paradise, with her Parma violets, her gold hair and floating scarves, among the austere black and white nuns and us drab, navy-blue clad schoolgirls. All kinds of romantic stories floated around about her: once, I remember, the story was that she had lost her voice because a man who shot himself for love of her had died at her feet. She had come to be consoled by Mother Clement. All of this created an aura of the great world, full of dangers, temptations and excitements, far removed from the daily grinding for public examinations and weekly examinations of foolish schoolgirl consciences. She was a living example of the glamour an old girl could attain to. In Dublin now in the fifties she and Kate O'Brien had many a talk in the lounge of the Shelbourne Hotel. I have no doubt she is the model for Rose Lennane in *As Music and Splendour*.

Of the model for the other Irish girl, Clare Halvey, who is associated with Rose Lennane all through the novel, we cannot be so certain. For the kind of voice she has and temperament, which is not operatically inclined, Kate O'Brien probably had a contemporary of Burke-Sheridan in mind, Margaret Lydon, and not, as has been suggested, Catherine Hayes, the great Limerick singer of an earlier age. Catherine Hayes figures in the novel, but as an historical character. For the details of Clare's nature and temperament, Kate O'Brien, not having a model to observe, had to rely on invention.

The period depicted in the novel is the late 1880s: the author has retreated to the Victorian era, in time a couple of decades later than the opening years of *Without My Cloak*. Her two young heroines, Rose and Clare, have been pitch-forked out of their homes and family in Ireland and sent to Europe to be trained as singers. They are both penniless and have been sent out into the world as a sort of investment by knowledgeable people at home. They are first entrusted to a rather dingy convent, the sole claim of which to distinction is the music mistress, Mère Marie Brunel and then, without warning, suddenly bundled off to Rome to the freer life of students, living in the household of their singing *maestro* and his wife. Their arduous and dedicated life is described in detail, the characters of their fellow-students sketched in, and the peculiar household of the *maestro* and his preposterous wife, Vittoria, suggested in a few deft strokes.

Thus Rose and Clare find themselves in an unusual position for girls of their time. Not only will they be educated musically, but they will be taught a variety of European languages and trained to behave suitably and gracefully on all social occasions. When they have finished their training, they will be in a way to earn a handsome livelihood, if not to become positively wealthy. Meantime they are free to order their own lives in a manner impossible for most girls of the period. One has only to think of Gissing's Ida Starr in *The Unclassed* (1884) or Thackeray's Becky Sharp in *Vanity Fair* (1848) to realize in what a privileged position their gift of a singing voice has placed these girls.

In short, Rose and Clare, already as students in Rome, have a measure of that freedom the pursuit of which is the preoccupation of all of Kate O'Brien's heroines. They are not consciously in pursuit of love as it is known in the adult world: both of them had been children emotionally when they were taken from their humble Irish homes: their love had been given to their relations, Rose's to her mother and little sister, Aggie, Clare's to her grandmother. They had both found their homesickness in Paris hard to bear. But as one summer follows another without their being allowed to return to Ireland, each has begun to feel the need of someone to love. Rose, whose career is advancing more rapidly than Clare's and whose kind of beauty and warmth of disposition, we are told, makes her almost irresistible to men, admits to herself that her life now would depend, as it had in childhool, on love, the 'love that she had to give as she had to breathe, and the love she had to take.' But she is in no hurry: she is in search of no 'protector', no wealthy old patron of the opera. She would 'plunge when she had the gift of her own free will, her own desire in her hands.' Now in the summer of 1889, two years after her arrival from Paris, she is singing with an unknown, young French tenor, René Chaloux, and after their first night together in *I Puritani* they become lovers, Rose doing the choosing.

Clare, who from time to time rebels against her destiny, finding in most of the roles offered in opera something absurd, and not wanting at all to use music to express her temperament, to exploit her 'unimportant, transient talent', but to serve music, to sing it exactly as the composer wrote it, would like to devote all her energies to oratorio and sacred music. She has a more austere, more complex, more difficult, less adaptable, less easily satisfied temperament than Rose. Yet it is she who breaks the rules under which they have both been brought up far more drastically than Rose. She and the Spanish girl, Luisa Carriaga, who had also been a pupil at the Paris school, become lovers for a time. This happens after they have played the leading roles in *Orphée et Eurydice*, as if the myth which they were enacting on stage had taken over their lives. But Luisa is not endowed with a faithful disposition; moreover, it is the nature of their calling that they must move around wherever there is a demand for their singing, so Clare and Luisa soon part. The author does not attempt to examine why the austere Clare, who says that, if she had been left at home, she would probably have become a nun, should allow herself to be so much greater a rebel against normal morality than Rose. It is never a question of Clare disliking or fearing men: in fact she enjoys their company and two of them, her fellow-student, the Welshman, Thomas Evans, and the Irish ex-seminarist, Paddy Flynn, appear to be in love with her. At the end of the novel Clare is on her way to Germany to join Thomas, who has dedicated a song-cycle to her, and will now be her *maestro*. Where Rose is concerned, it is made clear that it is she who decides to become René's lover: in both instances the point would seem to be that where women are socially free it is they who do the choosing. And they choose to end as well as begin. Rose's feeling for René does not last long. Antonio da Luca soon succeeds him in her affections, but when Rose learns that Antonio, who is represented as a member of a noble family, has calmly agreed to an arranged match, so that he may inherit his uncle's property, she ends the relationship. She will not injure the young girl who is going to be Antonio's wife.

I think the point Kate O'Brien would have made openly, if she had drawn her material from the Ireland of her own time, is made indirectly here in this story of two Irish girls set free in the 1880s of the last century, in the Italian world of opera by their possession of a remarkable soprano voice. Young, ardent, gifted, trained in a demanding art, and self-supporting from an early age, they make it clear that love for them is a gift of the self to another, uninfluenced by considerations of social class, pecuniary advantage or material comfort. The woman must be as free to choose as the man. She will take a lover, but not become anybody's mistress, nor agree to an arranged marriage. Love as a free movement of the human spirit and not as a part of a legal bond or as an assuagement of physical desire is in question here. Such an experience does not bring happiness, but the authorial comment of *Mary Lavelle*, 'woe to the sunless heart that has never been its dupe', holds good here too. These two girls break the moral laws they have been brought up in but they have their own sense of morality. Rose will not continue to be Antonio's lover when once she knows he is engaged to be married to an innocent young girl, and Clare is quite frank with Thomas about her love for Luisa.

As Music and Splendour is eminently a romantic novel, if we take Robert Louis Stevenson's definition of romance as our criterion:- 'the right kind of thing should fall out in the right kind of place', but the narrative impulse that had lifted and swung other stories along has slackened and weakened here. The writing as a whole is laboured, and the description of the various journeyings of the singers throughout Italy can seem repetitious. Sometimes the old skill shows itself, as in the account of Rose Lennane's triumph as Desdemona in *Otello*, reminiscent of Marguerite Burke Sheridan's triumph in *Madame Butterfly*, about which Puccini, when he asked himself how she could have sung so as to make him see things in his own music he had not realized were there, said that she could only have done it because she came of an 'old race full of dramatic temperament and spiritual vision'. But the general level is not on this standard, and there is another anomaly in a novel of realistic characterisation, the inclusion of caricature. The *maestro's* wife, Vittoria, can only be interpreted in this way. I have sometimes wondered if in this character Kate O'Brien intended a caricature of herself as she grew older.

Life in Connemara was not turning out to be the ideal it had seemed at first. The place was too isolated, offered too few engagements for the active intellect. It was easy to fall into a routine of good fellowship which involved the too frequent and too long continued lifting of the elbow. Financial problems grew threatening. The American performances of the dramatized *That Lady* had not brought in the money expected: *The Flower of May* had not sold very well. In the character of Vittoria, who presents us with a figure of declining ambitions, combined with 'art neglected, but when as now picked up for a lazy moment, still gold, pure gold', we are perhaps justified in seeing a picture of the author herself in her declining years. But we may also see embodied a universal problem for the artist, the gap between what seems attainable and what actually gets done. Kate O'Brien was very much an artist in this respect: she was sometimes tormented to frenzy by the problem, of how, as Shelley said:– 'Inspiration is a fading coal.' Vittoria is not the only artist who dissolved the problem in the anodyne of alcohol.

Whether I am right in this suggestion, or not, in the event *As Music and Splendour* proved to be her last novel. It was published in 1958. She lived until 1974, but published no further studies of the Irish girls in search of love and freedom. She did not stop writing. A travel book, *My Ireland*, was published in 1961 and a book of reminiscences, *Presentation Parlour*, in 1962.

PART 2

X

FOREIGN SETTINGS

When she was a young woman, Kate O'Brien spent the best part of a year in Spain: she went there as a 'Miss', a governess, to teach the children of the wealthy de Areilza family of Bilbao, one of whom, José Maria, was to become Foreign Minister after the accession to power of Juan Carlos. She fell in love immediately with the Spain she found, not the tourist Spain of red geraniums, clicking castanets and blazing sun, but northern, Basque Spain, of hard-working men and women, with a climate rather like that of Ireland, much given to rain and mud, where the 'strange sky gleamed with a familiar tenderness'; and later on with the Spain of austere Castile, of the great gold plain and the high, immaculate sky. Summer after summer in the early thirties she returned to the country until the Spanish War put an end to all such jauntings. A year after the outbreak of that war, in 1937, she published *Farewell Spain*, a travel book in which she expresses such anti-Fascist views that Franco banned her from the country for over twenty years.

Spain gave her the setting for two of her novels, one, her third work, *Mary Lavelle*, the theme of which belongs in the purely private sphere and deals with the psychosexual development of a young girl, the heroine who gives her name to the book, the other, a novel of sixteenth-century Spain, *That Lady*, in which the theme is the corruptive influence of absolute political power, the manner in which it vitiates private relations and the heroic resistance of a private person, who happens to be a woman, to the despotism of the ruler.

Mary Lavelle is depicted, at the time of her arrival in Spain, as a gentle, modest girl, rather passive in general, though she has been strangely determined to take this job as a Miss: at home she had fallen into the role expected of her as eldest daughter of the house, trying to please her peevish father and sycophantic Aunt Cissy, who had run the house since the death of her mother. Mary had also lived up to the normal expectations of her time by getting engaged to be married to a suitably masterful young man, to whom she has every intention of being a good wife, when he decides he has sufficient income to provide comfortably for them both. It seems but a whim that she insists on going to Spain for a year. Indeed, it seems not much more than that to herself: she hardly knows her own motives. The author, however, has hinted at these by telling us of Mary's childhood wish to live alone and be free to travel; her subconscious needs are other than those found on the trodden path beaten out by so many before her. She has not enjoyed being kissed by the masterful John.

Mary feels at once familiar with her new surroundings and at the same time homesick for her native town, Mellick. She is undergoing that sense of dislocation which the first experience of finding oneself removed from one's usual environment produces. The girl realizes with a shock that she is now a responsible adult, in charge of others. She is between two worlds:-

Mellick, where she lived and had left her heart, where she would live again and die, was remote and cloudy in this minute — out of focus, as assuredly this actual view was also, since nothing could in twenty-four hours have grown as clear and intimate as it suggested itself to be.

The view induces the eyes, she finds, but does not compel them:- 'It had no proclamation in it. In that it was surprisingly like Mellick.'[1]

In this description of her heroine's first reaction to Spain, where the foreign scene reminds her of her native one, Kate O'Brien shows her ability to analyse shadowy, dimly realized states of mind and emotional experiences not understood by those undergoing them. The Spain to which Mary Lavelle has come is the Spain of the Atlantic coast, so it is not surprising that she should find a confusing resemblance between it and her own part of the world near the Irish Atlantic. In a way her simplicity is shown by her being slightly thrown off balance by this. She goes on to think that in Spain she will be 'unobserved, uncherished' and, she hopes, 'unreproved.' She has, she believes, 'put on a cap of invisibility.' The irony of this is made immediately apparent by the response of Don Pablo, her pupil's father, to her physical appearance. For Mary Lavelle's appearance is startling: she is beautiful beyond all expectations, and Don Pablo finds in her, as we have seen, the old poetic myth of girlhood . . . untouched, unaware, unflirtatious, courteous — an unassuming governess-girl . . . looking about her with interest on a new scene and quite unaware that her brilliant beauty ravished the evening and rendered a sceptical and easily mannered man, her respectable employer, unable to utter more than one or two banal sentences before he hurried away in fear from his sudden senile folly.[2]

This is a prefiguring of the effect she is to have on a great many others, on the Misses, whom she meets when she has her free afternoon, those older Irish exiles, battered, poor, aging, proud and independent, vulgar and absurd, refusing to learn Spanish properly, insisting on their dignity, longing for Ireland but unable ever to afford to return. On one of them her effect is catastrophic: the bitter, self-contained Agatha Conlon responds to Mary's beauty and personality in such a way that she is gravely rebuked for it by her confessor: she is told that her feeling for Mary is wrong and sinful.

The Misses provide Mary with a new experience: she finds herself, for the first time, among wage-earning women, all considerably older than herself, all eking out a precarious living which leaves them permanently lonely, unimportant and unamused, too poor to be decorative, and entertaining for one another no more than a rough *camaraderie* which grotesquely imitates the unsentimental attitude of men thrown together, even to their calling one another by their surnames. Some of them, however, are still like young girls, naïvely dreaming of a husband, 'adoring you and giving you all kinds of gorgeous things'. One might expect that the effect of this on Mary would be to reinforce her feeling for John and the assured future he promises her. After all, as she reflects, these colleagues of hers are unexpected, admonitory figures, 'as full of morals and inferences as the Church Tower across the square'. The Misses show up as a foreign colony, strangely uninfluenced by the country of their adoption. With the exception of Agatha Conlon, they are in Spain, but not of it. They are, in fact, exiles. Mary is not.

It is Agatha who takes Mary to her first bullfight. As it happens, she sees there a great matador kill his bull with masterly skill, and is carried outside of herself. She sees the bullfight as savage, inexcusable, fantastic, but at the same time as more

vivid with beauty and beauty's anguish, more full of news of life's possible pain and senselessness and quixotry and barbarism and glory than ever before encountered by her, more real and exacting . . . more symbolic, more dramatic, a more personal and searching arrow to the heart than ever she dreamed of . . .. Here was art in its least decent form, the least explainable or bearable. But art unconcerned and lawless.[3]

In other words, Mary has had, in the bullfight, a revelation of the possible pain of life but also of its possible control through attitude, through the formalization, the distancing and patterning of art. Her experience of the bullfight becomes a symbolic representation of the advent in her life of the mysterious pain and ecstasy of love, rendered hopeless of any ordinary outcome by the circumstances of the young man who falls in love with her.

This is, as we have seen, Juanito, Don Pablo's son, the darling of his father, mother and sisters, trained to become one of 'Spain's great men', happily and brilliantly married, already the father of a son. The impossible, unwelcomed but irresistible love between the heir of the house and the unassuming governess-girl forms the nub of the book, but Mary learns also that family relations can be very different from those she has been accustomed to in her own home. The admiring love for Juanito, felt by everyone, is only part of the affectionate network which binds the Areavagas together. Don Pablo's concerned, gently ironic attitude to his three daughters is in marked contrast to her own father's bored impatience with his children. Mary's father's house, in fact, has not been a happy home for her. It had been made tolerable by the companionship of the brothers nearest to her in age, both of whom, however, unable to endure their father's peevish ill-will, had left home, and by the realization that she was soon to become John's wife and have a house of her own. But not until she came to Spain has she had any experience of what the life of a happy, united family could be.

Mary Lavelle, taking stock of herself, may well say that she is 'racing fast out of heedlessness'. She tries to mock herself out of her feeling for Juanito, telling herself that she is merely suffering, rather belatedly, from a schoolgirl crush, that he does not mean anything by the tragic eyes he has been making at her. But his actions make clear that he is as attracted to her as she is to him. Soon they acknowledge their love for each other, but Mary, reminding him that they are in a hopeless, insoluble muddle, that they are both Catholics, that there is no such thing as divorce — even if he wanted it — for Catholics and that there can be no furtive existence for her as his mistress, decides that she must leave Spain and return to Ireland.

Her whole life will be changed, she knows. She cannot now marry John, but she can better endure her pain at home in her own country.

On the eve of her planned departure, Juanito makes a characteristic re-appearance and drives her up into the hills above Altorno. There Mary makes a decision and says to him:-

Listen, it's been fantastic, my time in Spain. It's been a mad, impossible thing dropped into my ordinary life. Tomorrow it will be over, and although it has changed all my plans, life will have to be ordinary again in some way that I know nothing about now. So, before it's over, finish it for me, Juanito. I can't see how I can ever care for anyone again — I love you so much. I suppose I will — when I'm old and ugly. But I want you to have me first — just for this one time, up here where you used to play when you were a little boy. Nothing else will content me, however long I live, if you refuse me this.[4]

This one occasion will have to do her for life, she tells him, she will never make any claims on him, she takes all responsibility and all risks. And so, lawlessly, deliberately, Mary's virginity is given to Juanito. She breaks all the rules of her upbringing.

One can see why the novel was banned in Ireland. What shocked our moral guardians was not so much that here was a flagrant instance of sex outside marriage, but that the girl was not hounded into it, that she was the one to choose, that she knew her lover was married, but she had deliberately, from their point of view, wrecked her whole life, that she had taken the shadow for the substance. Well-brought-up Irish girls did not behave like this, or if they did, other Irish girls must not hear about it.

In fact what Kate O'Brien does in this novel is show a girl grow to womanhood, grow to an awareness of the nature of love and of life, once she has got away from the circumstances of her restrictive upbringing. Spain was chosen as the field of this development. We learn to define ourselves by contrast and comparison as well as by self-analysis. Mary had been set on the road to the unexamined life. She was engaged to be married, but did not love the young man who was to be her husband. She understood nothing about the nature of love. She thought it was a manageable feeling, by means of which one made life pleasant for other people. She had no under-standing that it is a cataclysm of one's being, as much a disruptive as a binding force. She did not know that it is the freely bestowed gift of one's self to another. But she learns. She learns in Spain, how-

ever, in circumstances which have no happy, conventional outcome.

Spain, it seems to me, was chosen, not merely because Kate
O'Brien knew the country well, but because Spain, like Ireland,
was a Catholic country. Whatever happened to Mary Lavelle there
could not be ascribed to the customs of a 'pagan' country. One pre-
sumes that the censors of the day knew that the Mediterranean
Catholic churches took a more lenient view of sins of the flesh than
did the narrowly Puritanic Irish Catholic church of the time, but no
doubt they would have considered that dangerous knowledge for
the flock.

Spain in this novel is not just a geographical place: it is an interior
landscape which provides crucial experiences in the development of
an Irish girl. Kate O'Brien makes no moral issue out of the
behaviour of her heroine; she remains detached, but behind it lies a
question. Is it better for Mary Lavelle to learn the real nature of love,
even though she sins against her Catholic training in so doing, than
to sleep-walk amiably into a marriage, agreed to but not desired by
her? Spain sets up contrasts, frees the individual from the constric-
tions that family expectations and social mores impose at home,
allows a young girl, by virtue of the chance that she is earning her
own living, to experience love, and thus grow in knowledge of
herself and human life. Spain, in short, is an arena which reveals the
extremes of possibility that life contains, instead of the narrow paths
of conformity which conditions at home had indicated.

In *That Lady*, published ten years after *Mary Lavelle*, Spain is
again used analogically, this time sixteenth-century Spain of the
time of Philip II. It is now made the scene of a drama of conscience
which is not confined to the private sphere of life but engages the
political world at the highest level. The years when Kate O'Brien
was writing *That Lady* were, as already mentioned, the years of the
Second World War, when the Nazi domination of Europe and all
that that entailed of crime against the rights of the individual and the
private conscience was being desperately opposed. In her fable here
she has an earlier example of tyranny trampling on the rights of the
individual. In the person of Philip II she explores the temperament
of one whom power corrupts, who confuses public might with private morality, who finds in what he considers an offence against his
own feelings an excuse for barbarous public punishment. In Ana de
Mendoza, Princess of Eboli, the most aristrocratic of Spanish

ladies, descendant of centuries of Spanish nobility, heiress to vast tracts of land and uncounted possessions, she gives us a heroine who almost by chance becomes the champion of the rights of the individual to order his private life as he chooses. Philip is depicted as having entertained a dog-in-the-manger affection for Ana and as liking to toy with the idea that, had it not been for his virtue, she would have been his mistress. As a great heiress, Ana had been the greatest matrimonial prize in Spain. Philip had 'given' her to Ruy Gomez, his First Minister. Because he loved and trusted Ruy, he would not tarnish what he had given him. Ana, for her part, had always liked the King, and as a little girl had thought it was he whom she was destined to marry. Her trust in him is to prove a factor in her undoing. Philip is to act as if a private sin were a public crime.

When Ana, now a widow, is visited by the King at her country estate of Pastrana and half-entreated, half-ordered to return to Madrid, she meets again the man promoted to Ruy's place, a former pupil of her husband, Antonio Perez. Almost as a whim, we feel, perhaps to exercise for the first time in her life a sexual choice, she takes him as her lover. The King's morbid feelings are exacerbated when he hears this news, and he cleverly and maliciously uses the intrusion of the half-mad, treacherous Juan de Escovedo in Antonio and Ana's affairs to have Antonio implicated in the subsequent murder of Escovedo, a murder exacted by him as a duty from Perez. In order to fan public suspicion he will not allow the matter to come to open trial.

Ana and the King engage in a battle of wills. She steadfastly refuses to concede that he has the right to her in private matters and send him insolent messages, making clear her support for Perez. He disguises his personal chagrin and jealousy under the pretext of reasons of state, and Ana is gradually deprived of everything. Perez escapes to France, and because she receives him on his flight there, she ends her days bricked-up in a couple of rooms in her country house, deprived of the sight of the sky, of freedom to move or communicate, with nobody for company except her youngest child, Anichu, who refuses to leave her and whose existence the King apparently overlooks. Ana dies in full communication with the Church. She had long repented of her sin: indeed she had begun to do so before Perez fell into disfavour with the King, but thereafter had been torn between her sense of religious obligation and her

aristocratic sense of obligation to a fellow-human being whose fate
had become bound up with hers. What had begun as mere carnal
desire had changed into lasting concern for another's welfare on her
part, and, on his, a faithfulness in love he had not known himself
capable of.

Once again it is Spain that is chosen as the scene of human
development, and once again it is a woman who is the protagonist
and who serves as vehicle of this development. Ana is both victim
and hero, physically a victim but spiritually a hero. I think she may
be seen in two lights, in a universal light, where she may be
regarded as typifying the lot of most women in a patriarchal society:
for all her wealth, her aristocratic descent and her powerful relations,
Ana is helpless against the despotic, neurotic King and is totally
isolated in her stand for freedom of choice in private life. In the
second interpretation, the novel may be read in application to the
years when it was being written and Ana be taken as an example of
the many men and women who, in defence of freedom, defied the
assaults and tortures of the Fascist régimes, whether in Spain, or
Germany, or Italy. As in these private dramas, here too great events
occupy the background: great personages move across the stage.
Europe is at war, or threatening war; the Armada sails and sinks;
plots to rescue Mary Stuart blaze up and fizzle out; William of
Orange is assassinated. But at the centre is a lonely woman, dying
of the illness induced by tyrannically imposed suffering and privation.

Kate O'Brien was banned from Spain for many years because of
what she wrote about Franco and his followers in *Farewell Spain*.
That Lady was not banned in Ireland, and perhaps the setting in
Spain, in the sixteenth century, was a deliberate strategy to avoid
such banning. The book was a triumphant success, both critically
and financially. Naomi Royde Smith described it as the work 'in
which Kate O'Brien has finally reached pre-eminence in her art and
must now be hailed as first among English women novelists.' But
I feel that *That Lady* was in a way a step sideways, that the banning
of *Mary Lavelle* and of *The Land of Spices* deflected her from doing
what she might otherwise have done, show a mature Irish woman
defy the narrow conventions of her day in Ireland and follow the
promptings of her heart, write a novel which, like the great
European novels of the time, questioned the most fundamental
values of life. But what, she must have felt, was the point of using
her own people in a contemporary setting to say what she had to say

about life, if her own people were not allowed to read her? She had to convey her convictions obliquely.

That she resented being banned in her own country is clear from *Pray for the Wanderer*, in which the London-based playwright, Matt Costello, is clearly a persona of the author: that she disliked intensely the claustrophobic, complacent, in-grown, Puritanic society that had developed in Ireland in the thirties and forties of this century is equally clear from this novel. 'A-holier-than-thou' attitude was anathema to her. When Ireland cuts herself off from Europe, she seems to suggest, this is what happens, this narrowing of interests and sympathies, this self-righteous officiousness. This modern, ostentatiously Catholic Ireland seemed not to know that ignorance is not innocence, that without freedom to choose there can be no virtue, that the sinner as well as the saint must be included in the community, that Christianity, to be Christianity, must include, must, perhaps I should say, embrace the sinner — 'condemn the sin but love the sinner' to use the time-honoured phrase. In other words, what was lacking in the Ireland was charity. Mrs. Grundy ruled in her stead. Only a bowdlerised version of life could be tolerated in literature. And this in a country where generation after generation of Catholic university students were required to read Newman's *The Idea of a University* in which it is clearly laid down that literature concerns itself not with men as they ought to be, but with men as they are, and whatever they do — *quidquid agunt homines*.

Since she could not use Ireland to show the development of the free spirit, she chose Spain, poor Spain, philosophic Spain, Spain which in the great plain of Castile, with its pale-gold distances and its 'passionately transparent' sky, seemed to offer an image of the purity of Paradise. She had no interest in — in fact, an active dislike of — Moorish Spain. She used to get quite angry with me when I would argue that one could not dismiss the Arab contribution to Spain out of hand; that the Arabs had had a highly sophisticated civilization and had contributed much of beauty to the architecture of Spain and had influenced the development of Spanish poetry. 'Let anyone who wants to interest themselves in the Arab contribution to Spain, do so', she would say. But don't ask her to do it. Christian Spain was what concerned her.

Kate O'Brien was, like many another Irish man or woman, a born traveller. Young people sometimes today forget that she was born a British subject. Ireland then was still part of the British Empire, to every part of which the citizen was free to travel. She never felt herself an exile in Europe or Britain. She went to England to look for a job after her graduation, because that was what every ambitious person with no clear career-pattern ahead of them did at the time. When in 1950 she bought a house in Ireland, she did so, as I have said, as an investment of some of the money earned from *That Lady*. She hesitated a long time about it and after ten years in Ireland returned to England to live. This was a free choice: she was not obliged to do so. There is no point, therefore, in fabricating a sentimental legend about her as an exile. She belonged to the world of writers and artists who traditionally are at home any place where they may live in peace and practise their art.

Just as she did not feel an exile abroad, but lived naturally in whatever country she happened to be in, so she did not use foreign countries to add local colour or some other frilly trimming to her novels: they are used organically and become part of the meaning of the work. Spain, especially, offers her a way of representing the tragedy and difficulty of life, the exploration of which lies at the core of her best novels.

And Spain could, in many ways, be used as a point of reference for Ireland. Both countries were Catholic, undeveloped materially, tenacious of ancient customs, politically troubled, anarchic in spirit, and both made a cult of death. But Spain was willing to acknowledge the irrational elements in human life and to absorb human passion into the fabric of life, while Ireland was at the time Jansenistic, Puritanic, almost Manichean in temper, a phase that her previous history and subsequent development would seem to point to as uncharacteristic. It was perhaps fortunate for Kate O'Brien that she came to know Spain so well: it offered her metaphors for meaning that otherwise might have been difficult to convey.

Mary Lavelle may be taken as Kate O'Brien's *bildungsroman*, in which the spiritual and emotional development of the heroine is traced. For all relevant purposes this heroine is a child when we first meet her. The various stages of her growth to maturity are delicately but clearly sketched, from her early shock of recognition that she is now an adult, not only in charge of her own life but responsible for others, her encounter with the other Irish Misses who represent the first wage-earning women she has ever met, her discovery of how different relations can be within a family from those in her own, and her attendance at the bullfight, which gives her a first apprehension of the power of art to control experience, to her falling in love and coming to understand that love alters one's whole perspective of life. Her time in Spain is short, but it will inform the remainder of her days.

The Land of Spices, though its present is set in Ireland, has as heroine a nun whose education has been wholly European. Since a considerable portion of the novel is concerned with the childhood, girlhood and young adult life of the nun, we hear in retrospect much about her education. As a child and young girl, she had attended the convent of La Compagnie de la Sainte Famille in Brussels, but her education has been carefully supervised by her English father, a specialist on the Metaphysical Poets of the seventeenth century. He had planned a university career for her in History and had proposed to take her on a tour of the great Italian cities after her final year at school. Her horrified discovery of her father's homosexuality changed all that. She became a nun and her entry into the convent meant her removal to Bruges, to the novitiate of the Order. Thereafter she is posted to various European cities until she returns to Brussels to act as Assistant to the Mother-General, before being sent to Ireland as Reverend Mother of the Irish convent of the Order.

The emphasis of this French-founded Order is on the training of girls in the Christian virtues of *la pudeur et la politesse,* but their intellectual development is not neglected; public examinations are taken and those who wish to are encouraged to prepare for university. The same Order and the convent in Brussels figure in a later novel, *The Flower of May*, with the same old Mother-General, Mother Gertrude, a mixture of shrewd worldliness and tolerant holiness. She assumes a life-long bond between the Order and every girl educated in its houses, unshocked, though grieved, by any particular girl's loss of faith, and utterly convinced that the Order will survive, with its aims unchanged, whatever upheavals Europe's political masters have in mind. She is thoroughly sympathetic to the ambitions of girls like Lucille and Fanny in *The Flower of May* and prepared to take Lucille's part, in her desire for a university education, against her formidable father. It seems as if the education offered by La Compagnie de la Sainte Famille, at once Catholic and liberal, represents an ideal for Kate O'Brien.

In *The Land of Spices*, Mother Archer's consciousness of the

European basis of the education offered by the convent makes her impatient of the nationalist aspirations of the Irish of the time. What she fears is the danger to the Christian virtues and values threatening from a World War which all the signs seem to indicate and which she knows to be a pressing concern of Mother-General. Not that she wants to suppress nationalistic feeling or the cultivation of Irish interests: indeed, she has encouraged several of her nuns to study the Irish language, and it is taught in the school. But she finds it absurd that people like the young Chaplain should think that the way to advance Irish interests is to denigrate the European values which are shared by all Christians.

The intellectual standards of the Irish school are as high as those of the Brussels convent, and Anna Murphy wins a County Council scholarship to University College, Dublin, at a younger age than the average pupil. Mother Archer, like her Mother-General, is prepared to do battle for the sake of the further education of her pupils, and routs Anna's snobbish grandmother, with her objections to the higher education of girls and her ignoble plans for Anna's future. Her interest is in the girl's welfare and what she wants for herself, not in a possible recruit to the religious life, as the mean Mother Andrew MacWhirter believes. At the end of the novel Anna Murphy is set to depart for a University career, reaching the same point that Mother Archer had reached before she entered the convent. In a sense we might see Anna's career as continuing on the lines the nun would have taken, had she not discovered her father's proclivities. Mother Archer, at the end, is set to depart on the next stage of her career, the Mother-Generalship of the Order. Schooling of the kind imparted by La Compagnie de la Sainte Famille can lead to success.

In *The Flower of May*, the Dublin-born Fanny has been a pupil of the Compagnie de la Sainte Famille in Brussels and there she met the charming Lucille. Fanny's elder sister, Lilian, her mother and her Aunt Eleanor had all been pupils of the school. Eleanor would have liked to join the Order, but her sister's marriage to Fanny's father had meant her having to stay at home to look after their father. Thwarted herself, Eleanor decides to enable Fanny to return to Brussels and continue her education. She shows the same disinterested goodwill as do Mother Archer and Mother-General.

Fanny's holiday in Brussels, visiting Lucille, affords us another aspect of life there, the life of the immensely wealthy de St. Mellin family, with every possible comfort and luxury taken for granted, the Comtesse's notion of calamity being somebody in the family not well enough to eat a meal. Fanny enjoys the experience of such a life, but holds herself aloof from it: it seems like a fairy-tale compared with the austere decencies of life at home. When the de St. Mellins take Fanny with them to Italy, she moves deeper into the forest of enchantments, but knows it for what it is. Venice is an unimaginable wonder, an unfolding of one delight after another, but not a place to live in, she says. In Italy, too, she almost falls into the snares of the unscrupulous, elder de St. Mellin brother; so that Italy for her is filmy with the possibility of love. But Fanny's natural detachment and good sense carry her through, if not unscathed, far from seriously wounded, and she is able to put her knowledge of André to use later on. She is called home to attend the sick-bed of her dying mother, and has to hasten across Ireland to the West coast, where her mother lies in the house of her childhood. She is hurried from the delights of a carefree holiday to the realities of family bereavement, from the man-made miracles of Italian cities to the wild beauty of nature on the coast of County Clare in her own country. Great grief awaits her, but unexpected good fortune in her Aunt Eleanor's generosity. Secure in the inheritance which has been bestowed on her, she chooses to kiss André: like Ana de Mendoza, in her widowhood, Fanny, in her new-found riches, feels free to choose. But the kiss is merely an expression of freedom, not of love, and Fanny's last dealings with André are in defence of her sister, not in pursuit of her own ends. Life in a French-speaking country and in Italy has brought Fanny from innocence to experience, has taken her a stage further in the education of her sensibility.

The Compagnie de la Sainte Famille appears again in *The Last of Summer*. Here the girl of the family, Jo Kernahan, has been at school in the Irish convent of the Order in Mellick and intends to become a nun. She has already acquired an M.A. at University College, Dublin, and been offered a Travelling Studentship, but the outbreak of the 1939 War has put an end to her hesitations and she is represented as trying to speed up her journey to the novitiate in Bruges: she would much prefer that to spending her days as a postulant in Ireland. The conclusion seems inescapable that the education provided by this French-founded, French-speaking Order represents for Kate O'Brien the best that Catholic education has to offer to girls.

In *As Music and Splendour*, Italy is the scene of the main action. The pair of heroines, Rose and Clare, are catapulted out of Ireland: they have been sent abroad with the minimum formal education because they have been discovered to possess rare musical gifts, voices of exceptional purity and power. After a preliminary stay in Paris to test these voices and ensure that they are as promising as they seem, they are just as precipitately dispatched to Italy. Ireland, thereafter, though they are for a long time desperately homesick, will never be their home again. Italy is to provide them with their education, an education in art and in social decorum and a field for the exercise of their gifts, the arenas where they find fame and earn a livelihood, where they develop from children to women, each going her own way and expressing herself in life, as in art, in a manner that would be, not just impossible, but unthinkable in Ireland. Rose climbs to fame more quickly than Clare: she becomes a *prima donna* after her performance as Desdemona in Verdi's *Otello* at *La Scala*. Clare makes her name more slowly as an exponent of sacred music.

Their training as singers is ruthlessly efficient: they are stretched to their limits, both mentally and physically. Rose has the temperament for opera; she enjoys the masquerade and the exploitation of self which it involves. All of this repels Clare; she thinks the roles which opera offer melodramatic and exaggerated to silliness. Her temperament is austere and solitary. Musically her desire is to be faithful to the score, not to use the music as an expression of her own personality. She and Rose sometimes talk about the wonder of finding themselves so well-educated. Both girls, by the accident of their musical gifts, are moulded by a European training into creatures they scarcely recognize as themselves. Italy, in *As Music and Splendour*, is not the land of the tourist or the dilettante, but of the rigorous professional, and Kate O'Brien shows an admirable knowledge of the studies and technique by which the professional expertise is acquired.

Italy is still, however, the land of love. For Rose to live is to love: what her career does is enable her to choose, just as Ana de Mendoza's widowhood does and Fanny's inheritance. She has her own standards of morality. She will take a lover, but forego him if he proposes to marry an innocent young girl and found a family with her. Clare is, ironically, the more radical of the two, and, unfortunately, we feel, for her happiness, she sets her love on another girl, the Spanish Luisa, bisexual and far from faithful. But Clare is loved by two men, the Irishman, Paddy, and the Welsh Thomas, and her musical future, we gather at the conclusion of the book, seems to lie with Thomas. The homosexual theme is very delicately handled. What Kate O'Brien wants to emphasise is rather the nature of love than its direction. Clare is the least promiscuous, the most austere and disciplined of all the young people in the novel. Love is love, the deduction seems to be, whether it is homosexual or heterosexual.

And Italy is still the country where the art of music is appreciated by the man in the street as well as by the connoisseur. In illustration there is the delightful scene of Clare and Thomas singing from Clare's window and being applauded from neighbouring windows. Italy is part of the theme of *As Music and Splendour*, the training of the artist.

In her first novel, *Without My Cloak*, the heroine, Christina, is shipped off to America by her aunt and Denis's uncle, Father Tom. That she is sent to America, the usual destination of the emigrant Irish, is a mere matter of expediency: if the next boat to leave had been to Australia, to Australia she would have gone. Denis goes in pursuit of her and spends the summer searching for her under the fierce, tyrannical sun of New York, pacing for hours between Broadway and the Bowery, down the wharves to the Battery, penetrating all the slummy streets of downtown New York, the sordidness and stuffiness of which are made the worse by the thought of the June just past, spent by the two of them in the cool meadow by the stream. Feverish from exhaustion and disappointment though he is, Denis often finds himself in sympathy with the life around him, with the sense of energy, vitality and expectation in the air and all the talk of gold. He sees the rawness but responds to the promise of this life, to the excitement of this incessant pursuit of money and power, all the lure of 'the clamouring, clattering, impressive and ridiculous town'. Just as the lyrical setting of Denis's and Christina's love was part of the magical quality of their feeling for each other, so the exhausting airlessness of New York is symbolical of the aridity that has dried up that love, as Denis suspects and proves true when at last he finds Christina, and they kiss, only to find that desire has died in them. Once again setting and meaning are woven together into the texture of the story. We have not only a remarkable evocation of the seedy side of New York, but a knitting of the description into the organism of the fable. We have romance and its failure, illusion and disillusion, figured out for us in place as in personal experience.

In short, Kate O'Brien never uses a foreign country for mere decoration or trimming: it always plays an organic part in the total design. As a result, we do not find stereotypes of foreign countries or of foreigners in her novels. Everything is seen with a fresh and purposeful eye.

XI

LOVE AND RELIGION

Kate O'Brien said in *Farewell Spain* that she was Catholic in all her blood. There are at least two of her novels the substance and conduct of the plot of which are bound up with the religious feelings of their respective heroines: these are *The Ante-Room* and *The Land of Spices*. Of *The Ante-Room* we can say more: the very pattern of the work, taut and trimly organized, is determined by the Church feasts of the three days at the end of October and beginning of November, days, of course, celebrated in the Celtic world long before Christianity, when the year turned from expansion and light to darkness and retraction; and, indeed, for almost everyone in the novel these three days portend nothing but a withdrawal of life and light. It is a sombre novel, but from the counterpoising of natural background, religious feeling and human suffering, a wintry poetry is distilled, at times muted, at others sparkling with frosty brilliance.

The occasion for all this is provided by the dilemma of a dying woman who wishes to be free to make her soul but is held to life by the need to continue to give moral support to her miserable son, Reggie. Belief in God's power, in the efficacy of prayer and the primacy of religious duties is taken for granted by everybody. Canon Considine, in ordaining the triduum of special prayer for his dying sister, is looking for a miracle, the prolongation of her life of suffering for her son's sake:- 'Perhaps God, who could do all things, would see fit to change the course of nature, or would quiet her troubled heart and compose it for death by revealing some scheme of safety and non-desolation for her son. And that would be a miracle.' For the poor, ineffectual husband and father, Danny, God is a household word:- 'When men talked of God he saw light. Doctors were mysteries.' Nothing was more natural for Agnes, we are told, than prayer, yet when the novel opens, Agnes has not been to the sacraments for months, and knows that she will not be able fully to take part in the triduum of prayer for her mother until she

113

has made a special effort to go to confession.

The three days are punctuated by religious services. Agnes goes to Evening Devotions and Benediction on the Sunday afternoon and stays after it is over to ask for a priest to hear her confession: the service moves her as it has since childhood, with the distinct voice of the priest, answered by the confused storm of responses from the congregation, thundering at Heaven's gate. Her examination of conscience is a model of orthodox procedure, following the traditional division into sins against God, against one's neighbour, against oneself. She is consoled and strengthened after she has received absolution and feels that she can now face the ordeal of meeting the beloved Vincent again. The great event of the next day, the Feast of All Saints, is the Mass in the house for her mother, attended by everybody, servants as well as members of the family, including Vincent. The following morning Agnes and Marie Rose go together to early Mass to pray again for their mother. But Agnes has been through terrible, scorching regions of the spirit since her confession on the Eve of All Saints: she has learnt that the armour of religion cannot defend her from love; that Vincent's hand on her shoulder has the power to suffuse her whole being with the realization of their mutual feeling; she has had the midnight meeting with him in the summerhouse where she had, after much discussion, suddenly understood that she could never go away with him, as he had suggested, because the figure of her sister, Marie Rose, stands between them. It is love that must overcome love; one kind of love must give way to another. She has confronted the fact that to love each other as Vincent and she do is a sin. She also feels that, as she tells him, 'in the end the Church is right, only we can't see it, well, transfigured. And I think we will, when we're dead.' But it is not religious scruple that determines the outcome for her; it is not reason or prudence; it is feeling of another kind, her love for her childhood companion, Marie Rose.

What then are we to make of the parade of religious feeling and religious ritual which forms so much of the substance of the novel? The point would seem to be, that no matter how sincere or intense the feeling, nor how well-observed the ritual and the duties, there is one experience which can set them at nought, 'one thing in the world', as Vincent says, 'which may be worth regrets and dishonours'. If we take this in conjunction with the remarks in *Mary Lavelle* about the glory, illusion though it be, of romantic love, where the authorial voice is heard, we may conclude that this is the author's own standpoint. In other words, love is that upheaval of the self which can destroy pre-suppositions and obliterate established patterns of behaviour. Certainly Vincent takes it to the last human frontier, the frontier between life and death.

There is a ferocious irony at the end of the novel, in that it is the prayers alone of the dying woman that are heard: she alone can say contentedly, 'God is good. Always he is good. He never fails us.' Love is her problem too, but it is maternal love; her anxiety about the wretched Reggie is met by the decision of the calculating, mercenary Nurse Cunningham to marry Reggie and look after him in return for financial security and material comfort. It is the least attractive characters in the novel whose affairs have been satisfactorily settled. God has arranged that Reggie should be looked after by a surrogate mother — Reggie who, as far as we can judge, has done least to deserve happiness and who has little or nothing to offer to life. God has also arranged things nicely for Nurse Cunningham, who is prepared to subdue emotional needs to material welfare.

In *The Land of Spices* religion is seen by the heroine as a refuge from self and the world. Helen Archer begins her adult life by making an egotistic use of religion, flying to the conventual life from the shock and disillusion of her discovery about her father. He has unknowingly wrecked her faith in human love, and she shudders away from all manifestations of earthly affection to set her thoughts on the pure and austere service of God.

As a nun, that service is fulfilled by teaching the young and leading them to an understanding of the Christian way of life. When the novel opens we find her suffering from dryness of spirit. She is haunted still by her inability fully to forgive her father, by her general fear of human feeling and by the discomfort of her present position, Reverend Mother of an Irish convent, but lacking in sympathy with Irish nationalist aspirations. Mother Archer is suffering a reaction to all the years of attempting to do violence to her human nature: her fear of love, even of the love of God, has produced her present condition of *accidie*. The progress of the story sees, first, her cautious admission of feeling for a particular human creature, the child Anna, whose innocence and receptiveness touches her heart and whose choice of poem brings back a flood of memories of her father, and then, gradually, her acceptance of the fact that she had no right to sit in judgement on her father, that God alone has the right to judge and to punish. We witness the slow and difficult moral development of the woman, her belated coming to terms with that from which in girlhood she had precipitately fled. The loneliness and mercilessness that her father had noticed on her return to Place des Ormes and had made him tremble, he says, for the young people in her charge, had long ago been recognized intellectually as a fault, but it is not until she allows herself once again to feel a spark of human tenderness that she can act on this recognition and open herself to human need in all its folly and irrationality. In the history of Mother Archer we witness a growth in moral stature: we see a good religious and skilled administrator develop as a spiritual being: we see her ultimate justification of the religious life as a way of opening the spirit to the highest reaches of virtue, to humility, to confidence in God's decrees, to the unceasing exercise of charity. When, at the end of the novel, Mother Archer is called to the supreme office of her Order and is summoned back to Brussels as Mother-General, we can feel that her private troubles have been resolved and she will be able to devote all her energies to the duties of her office.

This novel, like *The Ante-Room*, is punctuated by religious ceremonies, but they are celebratory ceremonies and are often followed by ordinary festive occasions. The opening scene is of the Reception of three postulants to the religious life. It is a joyful moment, as the Bishop remarks:- 'when people decide to give up the pride of life instead of planning to snatch it, I don't want to make heavy weather. I like to rejoice, since God rejoices.' The Bishop makes this remark at the Reception breakfast which follows the religious ceremony. The *Quarant Ore* Exposition of the Blessed Sacrament is another ceremony attended by particular formalities, beginning and ending with sung High Mass, and allowing certain girls the thrill of rising in the middle of the night for an hour's vigil before the Altar of Repose. On this occasion also the Convent's hospitality is exercised; lunch is served to the priests who celebrate the Masses. The last ceremony, which we do not witness but are told is about to happen, is the singing of the Te Deum in honour of Mother Archer's promotion to the Generalship of the Order: the singing of the Te Deum is the supreme expression of rejoicing in the liturgy of the Church.

In addition to the religious ceremonies, there are various other celebrations at intervals in the course of the novel: these, however, are connected in some way with religious events or characters. We only hear of Foundress's Concert, but Chaplain's Concert makes for the most entertaining chapter in the book. Only priests, or those shortly to become priests, are invited to this concert, and it is the mannerisms and peculiarities of their guests that enchant and excite the girls and lead them into perilous expression of folly and frivolity, both at the entertainment and at the supper-party that follows. The girls use the occasion and their guests, priests and seminarians, as an opportunity for exemplifying, to an exaggerated degree, their command of *la pudeur et la politesse*, the Christian lessons that the school sets out to inculcate in them. Everything in this concert, as in all other activities, is seen as in some way connected with religion. There are no ironies here. Anna Murphy is going on to university and Mother Archer to assume the supreme role of government in her Order.

Religion as a refuge for the bruised ego, religion as a moulder of character and conduct, religion as a sphere of moral development, and finally religion as offering a career with a scale of possible hierarchical advancement — all these aspects are implied in the progress of the story and the exploration of character in *The Land of Spices*. Yet there is no trace of anything pre-arranged for edification, which too often can be found in the 'religious' novel. At the other extreme we can marvel that such a novel should ever have been banned. It had been suggested by the ribald among us that our censors did not understand the import of the title, that they did not realize that it is one of George Herbert's metaphors for prayer and taken from the following sonnet:-

> Prayer the Churches banquet, Angels age,
> Gods breath in man returning to his birth,
> The soul in paraphrase, heart in pilgrimage,
> The Christian plummet sounding heav'n and earth;
> Engine against the Almightie, sinners towre,
> Reversed thunder, Christ-side-piercing spear,
> The six-daies' world transposing in an houre
> A kinde of tune, which all things heare and fear;
> Softnesse, and peace, and joy, and love, and blisse,
> Exalted Manna, gladnesse of the best,
> Heaven in ordinarie, man well drest,
> The milkie way, the bird of Paradise,
> Church-bells beyond the starres heard, the souls bloud,
> The land of spices; something understood.

In *Mary Lavelle* and *That Lady*, religion and its place in life is taken for granted. It does not prevent Mary from indulging her love for Juanito, but she accepts that, as Catholics, she and Juanito can have no future together, and, like Agnes, she proposes to remove herself from the source of temptation. Ana de Mendoza, when she is enjoying the pleasures of love, misses the consolations of religion and had intended to give up her lover and return to the practices of her faith until she is driven by Philip into feeling that her human obligations must take precedence over her obligations to God.

We should all agree, I suppose, that love is the one force that can rival religious feeling and that a conflict of interests between them is the most devastating and disorienting of sufferings. In Kate O'Brien's day, Irish bourgeois society did not acknowledge the possibility of such a conflict: it was taken for granted that all good Catholics firmly and successfully subjugated mere human affections to the dictates of their religion: sexual sin was the worst of sins: it seemed sometimes as if it were considered to be the only sin. Kate O'Brien surely did a service to that society by showing that 'good' Catholics, fully cognisant and acceptant of the teaching of their religion, could be torn in allegiance between human needs and religious duties, that to love, even where barriers are reared against the consummation of that love, does not make one a monster of depravity.

The religion that Kate O'Brien's characters profess is Roman Catholicism. She limits herself to the exploration of such a religious background, because that is what she is familiar with, what she knew from babyhood. She herself, as she tells us in a fragment of autobiography, 'lost the faith', as we say, while she was still at school: intellectually she became estranged from Catholicism but emotionally she remained attached to it. She was, as long as I knew her, an agnostic, but a 'Catholic agnostic', as the Dublin saying goes, and she died reconciled to the Church. She could, of course, theoretically, have written about a 'modern' Irish woman or man who had gone through the ordeal of loss of religious faith, someone who had either to continue to exist in a state of philosophic and spiritual uncertainty and suffer all the *angst* of such a state or to try heroically to work out an individual philosophic standpoint. But she did not attempt this. The reason must lie partly in the fact that she knew such a novel would be banned in Ireland: it would have had to go far in daring beyond anything she did write. She felt very much in sympathy with writers who do portray the modern experience of the senselessness of existence and the realization that, as Freud said, 'the aim of all life is death'. She recognized, at once, Samuel Beckett's quality and described him as a 'kind of desolate mystic'. She had a sustained admiration for the great Saint Teresa of Avila and what, in spite of life-long bad health, she achieved. She had a horror of old age, its indignities and diminutions, and the bleakness of facing the end without the comfort of old usages. She herself underwent the quarrel with the culture she grew up in that is found in most writers of any worth in modern literature, but she did not represent any such characters in her writings: the problems her heroines confront are not metaphysical or theological: they are existential and arise when the experience of living comes into conflict with the rules for living inculcated by their religion.

XII

TIME AND TECHNIQUE

The management of time is proverbially a difficulty for novelists. They must sometimes create an impression of the slow passage of time without boring the readers, sometimes, on the contrary, of its swift elapsing without being too laconic: occasionally they must set the sensation of the movement of time experienced by a particular character against the actual clock, or the calendar: in addition they may have to move backwards and forwards between the past and the present. We might sum up by saying time may be contracted, expanded, juxtaposed, or, as it were, re-created or remembered.

Kate O'Brien uses all these devices, and I think we find that in her more successful novels the skilful handling of time contributes much to their quality. In *Without My Cloak*, which, though long, maintains its hold on the attention of the reader throughout, she for the most part contracts time and concentrates on specific highlights in the family history, such as celebratory occasions, birthday parties, housewarmings and promotions, or on dangerous crises in their affairs, such as Caroline's attempt to run away from her husband. At one stage, however, she expands time: when Denis is searching for Christine in New York she has of necessity to show the persistence and tedium of his search, and so, these two months are given in detail disproportionate to the rest of the novel, and the perception of time is seen to be determined by the emotional condition of the perceiver. All of this is competently handled and we are made aware of the sensation of time as experienced in real life, the sense of its expansion or contraction, as we are bored and tired, or absorbed and happy.

In *As Music and Splendour*, however, these difficulties are not so well met. We accept naturally enough that the opening days in Paris for the two young Irish girls, lonely and confused as they are, must be long and tiresome: the description of their state is not tiresome. Afterwards in Rome when the pace might reasonably be quickened, there is too much pedestrian description and explanation, and the reader feels subjected to the same exhausting routine as the singers. The picnic on the Feast of the Assumption, which offers the kind of festive occasion that the author in earlier novels knew triumphantly how to bend to her purposes, fails of its effect and seems to be most sensibly spent by Vittoria, who falls asleep. I think this inelasticity, as it were, in the handling of time in *As Music and Splendour* is one reason why the novel seems to move so slowly. A steady walking pace is not the best mode of progress through a novel.

Where Kate O'Brien handles these temporal problems in masterly style is, I suggest, in *The Ante-Room* and *The Land of Spices*, in *The Ante-Room* by the device of expansion, and in *The Land of Spices* by alternating the flash-back technique and straightforward narration in order to move between the past and the present. In *The Ante-Room*, the town of Mellick, which we got to know so well in *Without My Cloak*, is at a distance, its affairs intimated only by the sound of bells. We are on the other side of the river and our attention is turned inwards, concentrated on the interior of the house and what is being enacted there. Agnes leaves the confines of the house or garden only to go to Church; doctors come and go; a sister and brother-in-law arrive on a visit; a priest comes to say Mass in the house. What movement there is is centripetal.

In this claustrophobic atmosphere the two and a half days of the action is measured off for us, not merely by the bells of Mellick, but by the hall-clock of Roseholm. Our attention is drawn to the exact time at which things happen from the hour when Agnes wakes up on the eve of the Feast of All Saints to the suicide of Vincent on the afternoon of the Feast of All Souls. Agnes wakes up at eight o'clock: between then and half-past ten she gets up and dresses, goes to see her mother, presides over breakfast, reads the letter that her father has received from Marie Rose (delivered, it seems, on Sunday morning — a rare slip on the author's part) and sees to various household duties. At half-past ten she has her usual daily interview with Dr. Curran — we are told that he came down the stairs as the hall-clock was striking the half-hour. She goes to twelve o'clock Mass and to Benediction in the Jesuit Church at half-past four. When she returns, Marie Rose and Vincent have arrived, and Marie Rose, complaining about her being late, tells her it is long after half-past six. The hall-clock strikes the quarter past seven before the two sisters come down to dinner, and the hall-clock is striking midnight as they go to their rooms to retire for the night.

And so with the next day: it too is carefully measured out by the bells of the various churches and the clock in the hall. We are told that midnight is striking in the town when Agnes goes out to the summerhouse to talk to Vincent; later, when all has been discussed between them, that two o'clock has struck. The account of the following morning begins as usual with an announcement of the time; and Vincent, before going to the summerhouse to shoot himself, carefully defines when it will all be over by asking Dr. Curran to come to him there as soon as he can after half-past one.

At first or second reading this careful notation of time may be missed, but let the attention once be drawn to it, and it can appear obsessional. The purpose, of course, is to make clock time appear protracted so as to correspond to the experience of Agnes, the long-drawn-out psychological ordeal that she is undergoing, the intensity of her suffering, the sense she has of being stretched and travelling through immense spaces of living: imaginatively she is on the rack every minute of these days, and the reader is stretched with her through the marked hours.

In *The Land of Spices* Kate O'Brien uses the device of the flashback to recreate the childhood of Mother Archer and her time as a young nun, in contrast to the 'present' of the novel, when she is the Reverend Mother of an Irish convent. It seems to me that this device, when it is well-handled, as it is here, effectively swings the imagination from one pole of interest to another. It can set up a contrast of background against background, character against character in different stages of development, and emotional tone against emotional tone. Here it enables the author to run in parallel Mother Archer's and Anna Murphy's career, though a generation separates them. Mother Archer's psychological loss of her father counterpoints Anna's loss of her brother by drowning, and Mother Archer is able to help Anna because she has herself suffered. Place can be brought close to place by means of this technique, convents in Bruges and in Brussels brought close to the convent in Mellick. Incidents in the present life of Mother Archer serve to recall naturally earlier events, and present and past merge into one another in the consciousness of the nun, as they do in the consciousness of us all.

The flash-back allows an author to by-pass mere chronological progression and make use of the involuntary memory, which can not just recall but recreate the past. The involuntary memory is often set in motion by the recurrence of some sense-impression, like the eating of the famous madeleine in Proust. In *The Land of Spices*, Mother Archer, hearing the child, Anna, recite Vaughan's poem, 'My Soul, there is a Country', is carried back to her own childhood. This device makes the presentation of experience more psychologically convincing than would straightforward narration. None of us lives only in the present, with an eye on the future: we are all Janus-facted, looking backwards as well as forwards; and quite young children can have lost worlds and territories which they have left behind them.

As well as the presentation of past and present there is in this novel an adumbration of the future. At the end Anna 'is for life', we are told, and Mother Archer is for the Generalship of her Order, with a Te Deum about to be sung in her honour. The book, for all the sorrow and suffering recorded in it, is optimistic; the future is, as we say, 'full of promise'. And this answers the expectations of the normal reader for whom the future is always full of promise, besides being limitless. The end of both *The Ante-Room* and *The Land of Spices* engages the imagination: we think with pity and horror of Agnes, as the news of Vincent's suicide is broken to her, and we dally with the possibilities open to Mother Archer and to Anna as a new phase of their existence begins for them. *Without My Cloak* is the only one of Kate O'Brien's novels that ends in the conventional manner of the Victorian novel, with a marriage in the offing. In most of the others a girl is left confronting her future: in *That Lady* a woman dies; in *Pray for the Wanderer* the hero leaves Ireland and returns to his accustomed life. Time ends or Time resumes.

In both *The Last of Summer* and *Pray for the Wanderer* the 'time' of the novel is an interlude, a break from usual life, or a holiday for the protagonist, 'time off'. Angéle in the one and Matt in the other are tempted to abandon the pattern of their lives and construct a new one. In the event neither does so. Neither finds the Ireland that they are visiting congenial, voluptuously beautiful though it is. They return to the mainstream of their lives and leave their holiday land for reality. In these novels this is what Ireland seems to have become for Kate O'Brien, a not altogether attractive holiday land. Here time and place are closely bound up. The time of the holiday draws to a close: the place is left. It is one way of imposing a pattern on material. One might say that in these novels Kate O'Brien is no longer a Great Auk writing for other auks: she is writing *about* them.

XIII
ROMANTIC ELEMENTS

The true novelist's attitude must be a detached one, we know, but nevertheless no novelist can escape an involuntary and oblique manipulation and predisposition of the reader's sympathies. We will naturally involve ourselves in the interests of the character whose story unfolds from within, at whose centre we find ourselves: we will be affected by choice of words, by the connotations of words, by the very title, by chapter headings. So, for instance, if we read:-
The Adventures of Philip on his Way through the World, showing Who robbed him, Who helped him, and Who Passed him by, we know we are supposed to be on Philip's side and to condemn those who are not. The implicit reference to the Good Samaritan carries all kinds of overtones. The Good Samaritan is an extravagantly romantic figure: he shows the warmest compassion to a complete stranger and the stranger has the romantic attraction of the innocent suffering undeservedly.

Kate O'Brien's titles are full of suggestiveness. Five of them come from verse or song, *Without My Cloak* from a Shakespeare sonnet, the significance of which the reader is all the time trying to determine, *Pray for the Wanderer* from the May hymn of that title, the relevance of which comes into view as the story develops, *The Land of Spices* from a difficult poem by George Herbert on prayer as the life of the spirit, *The Flower of May* from a sentimental song, the sentimentality of which is turned into irony by the heroine's progress, *As Music and Splendour* from the Shelley poem of that title in which the splendour of the product is set against the frailty of the vessel. Only one of the titles is straightforwardly descriptive, the name of the heroine, Mary Lavelle, being given to the book. The remaining three, *The Ante-Room, The Last of Summer, That Lady*, conceal their meaning until we are well advanced in the story, and *The Ante-Room*, in fact, allows of no one simple meaning: it may be explained in several ways. From the moment, therefore, of reading the title the reader's

124

interest and expection are aroused and he finds himself immersed, not in the ordinary world, but in the romantic world of heightened perception.

Kate O'Brien may also be considered a romantic novelist in that she can marry setting and incident in a strikingly appropriate way. To be convinced of this we have only to recall from *Without My Cloak* such a scene as Denis, after months of searching, at last finding Christina by the water's edge on the stuffy New York night, or his coming on the immaculate Anna in the rose garden while his twenty-first birthday party goes on without him in the lighted house. Or we may remember in *The Land of Spices*, Molly crucified, as it were, against the tree while Ursula de la Pole spits vulgar abuse at her, or the scene on the steps of the convent, geraniums foaming on either side, when Anna Murphy, attempting to explain *Lycidas* to pretty, frivolous Pilar, has the illuminating vision which reveals Pilar as herself a motif for art.

That Lady has many such moments, none more telling, perhaps, than that which shows the jealous King lurking in the shadow of the church porch to watch his victim, the Princess of Eboli, being taken from her palace and carried off, on his orders, to prison. We are not shown directly but merely told of the horrifying scene where Juan de Escovedo sneaks into the Princess's palace and violates the privacy of her bedroom, but the effect on the imagination is none the less vivid for that. *The Ante-Room* is full of this matching of setting and incident, Agnes at Benediction on the afternoon of All Hallowe'en, Vincent from the doorway listening to Marie Rose singing *Du bist die Ruhe*, Agnes going out in the freezing night of All Saints to meet Vincent and tell him they must part. Most of these scenes have Agnes as centre. There is scarcely a detail that is not laden with significance. When the book was published, practically every girl reader saw herself in the role of Agnes, torn between love and duty, and trembling in the frost as she went out to try to resolve her problem. But what really fixed the attention of such a girl was the realization that there never is a solution to a struggle between love and any other demand on the spirit, that a struggle of that kind puts its victim on a perpetual treadmill: and this realization is at once terrible and exalting; for, while it speaks of suffering, it also testifies to the power of the human spirit. The ending here is artificial: Agnes has the Gordian knot cut for her.

The power to create a character with whom the reader can sympathize is a gift of the romantic novelist: the incidents which absorb our attention and sweep us off into another world, as we say, must happen to or issue from a character in whose place we can put ourselves. The romantic writer appeals to the imagination, that power of the mind which sees so many more ways and means than can ever be realized in any one life, which temporarily restores choice to the will, which takes us out of the real, the narrow round of the self, and releases us into the free air of the not impossible. And, ironically, it is the imagination, so susceptible to glamour and enchantment, which is, nevertheless, the instrument of moral good, as Shelley said; for without the exercise of the imagination we cannot put ourselves in the place of another and feel compassion and sympathy.

It is, however, for the portrayal of the passion of love that the common reader describes a novelist as romantic, and the common reader is right. For love is the greatest agent of change that exists: love opens and closes vistas for all human beings; love forms and deforms; through love the world of human kind is held together and perpetuated; through love the human spirit is opened and irradiated. Kate O'Brien shows the operations of love in many different characters, from the naïve young girl, Mary Lavelle, to the guarded and austere Reverend Mother in *The Land of Spices*. She shows love delighting its devotees, torturing its victims, as Rose in *As Music and Splendour* or Agnes in *The Ante-Room*. She shows love as a deforming, egotistic passion in *That Lady* and *The Last of Summer*, as a youthful illusion or a frustrating deprivation in *Without My Cloak*. The place of love in her picture of the world might be summed up by Mother General Gertrude's remark to Mother Archer:- 'God is love, my daughter, and is served by love'. All her heroines are in pursuit of love and they are clear-sighted enough to realize that they must combine this with the pursuit of freedom.

Love, like all human emotions can be distorted, and the danger here is the corruptive power of jealousy which can turn love into a possessive smothering of, or debilitating clinging to, the beloved: we have examples of this in Hannah Kernahan and Anthony Considine. Romantic love is an idealising force that carries within it the seeds of disillusion, but an authorial interjection in *Mary Lavelle* expresses pity for the human heart incapable of it.

In the romantic writer love does not necessarily, or often, lead to happiness of a conventional kind. More often than not, it involves great suffering, but suffering and melancholy are also part of the romantic vision of human life. Only one of Kate O'Brien's novels — and that her first — ends, as I mentioned earlier, in the conventional Victorian manner, with the prospect of a happy marriage: perhaps even that is saying too much, since both Denis and Anna are 'difficult' characters. Perhaps we should say with the prospect of a marriage, which, however stormy it may turn out, will engage the energies of both parties.

XIV

CONCLUSION

The subject of feminism is never openly raised in Kate O'Brien's work. But the theme of her novels is the necessity for woman to be as free as man. When she was growing up, the modern feminist movement was in its beginnings and it is only now and gradually that the assumptions underlying the theory of man's superiority in the abstract and the facts of his legal superiority are starting to yield to the revolt of woman. When we consider how long was the rule of the laws that subjected woman to man, we should not be surprised at how slow is the change nor how resistant the opposition. 'Ancient Law subordinates the woman to her blood-relations, while a prime phenomenon of modern jurisprudence has been her subordination to her husband', says Sir Henry Maine in his great book *Ancient Law*. In later Roman law the Roman lawyers had devised numerous expedients for evading the old rules, but the revived barbarism of Europe in the Dark Ages combined with the emerging dictates of the Canon Law of the Christian Church to keep alive the disabilities of married women. In such a system love and freedom between the sexes had no part. A woman was a chattel, a moveable possession. Of course, law always lags behind the moral development of a people, but it is astonishing for how long endured the discrepancy between, on the one hand, the possibilities of feeling between men and woman and, on the other, the legal status of each. Europe saw the rise of the *amour courtois* of the Middle Ages, of the *femme maitresse* of the eighteenth century, and of the Romantic Movement at the end of the nineteenth century, while the legal status of woman remained unchanged.

When the modern feminist movement began at the end of the last century, it was natural enough that some of the strong-minded women who led or supported the movement should think that to prove themselves unfrivolous and the equal of men they should adopt some of their physical habits, like cutting their hair short and smoking cigarettes. The concept of 'equal but different' had not yet emerged. None of Kate O'Brien's heroines shows the least tendency to imitate men in this way. None of them is what used to be called, when I was a child, a tomboy. They merely want the essential conditions of life that men enjoy, the freedom to educate themselves, to develop what gifts of mind they have been endowed with and to gain from this education the qualifications to earn their living: only then can they make the free gift of themselves in love. Education is necessary even to make a case for women. Jane Austen, whose heroines are all brought into line with the conditions of their society, nevertheless has Anne Elliot say in *Persuasion*:- 'Men have had every advantage of us in telling their own story. Education has been theirs in so much higher a degree: the pen has been in their hands. I will not allow books to prove anything'.

It was also, I suppose, to be expected that the feminist movement in its early stages should result in some of its supporters believing that women might free themselves, even sexually, from men, by loving other women. What, in theory, could be more logical? In fact, it did not take long to discover that sexual bondage is bondage, no matter who the partners in the relationship are. Only one of Kate O'Brien's heroines shows any such inclination. This is Clare Halvey in *As Music and Splendour*, and there we are free to think that the myth of Orpheus and Eurydice has beglamoured her and Luisa, that they are working out in real life the roles they have taken on as artists. The result of this, as of most of the bonds of love in her novels, is unhappiness. Only in two attachments, that between Anthony and Mollie in *Without My Cloak* and between Will and Una in *Pray for the Wanderer*, do we see happiness resulting, and the first instance ends in the premature death of Mollie, because the rule of her Church laid down that there should be no artificial impediment to the fruits of sexual intercourse. Mollie dies of her ninth child.

The world of Kate O'Brien's novels is a sombre place, in the sense that men and women are shown as very rarely happy and when they are, but briefly. Her heroines, however, are the proof that she does not see happiness as the end of life. The end of life for women as for men is effort, achievement, the realisation of potentialities: it is love, not sexual satisfaction, and love is a gift that only freedom allows one to bestow. Sometimes her heroines achieve spiritual freedom in an environment that limits physical freedom, as her nuns do; sometimes spiritual freedom involves the complete loss of physical freedom, as it does for Ana de Mendoza. But this is the result of the arbitrary exercise of absolute power by a man who happens to be a sovereign ruler. Philip thought he loved Ana: his case proves that true love must allow freedom to the beloved.

Taking the word 'world' in a physical sense, we can see how responsive she is to natural beauty, to the skies, waters and light, the trees, growth and contours of whatever land she sets her story in. But when her own country is the setting, she has a magical ability to evoke in a few words the time of year, the kind of wind blowing, the quality of the air, and the mood created by such factors, from the soft, sweet-smelling evening breezes of the opening scene of *Without My Cloak* to the remembered dampness of Galway evenings in *As Music and Splendour*. She can do more than this: she can use the physical world to suggest some magical realm beyond the senses, as she does in *The Land of Spices*.

We may notice, if we refer to the passage from the novel quoted above (p. 66) that the landscape there is, as with the landscape of Somerville and Ross, presented as if animated with human feeling: it *lives* and *breathes*: the reflection of the sky is renewed in the *breast* of the lake, the hills *breathe* and *sigh*, the garden is *impassioned*, at *breaking point, feverishly poised, oblated*, the perfume of the wallflowers *troubles* the air, the fuchsia *foams* along the terrace. In short the evening in its natural aspects is described as if alive with human passion, but against this is set the pleasure *cries* of the boaters and bathers, as if they had been sated by the experience of the passion suggested by these manifestations of nature and are rebuked by the *tranquillity* of the trees and the *broad-based* house.

In *The Last of Summer*, the beauty of the Cliffs of Moher headland is used differently. Here are the relevant passages:-

The picnic was well set — in a stretch of brilliant turf, about fifty feet inland and downward from the very lip of the highest cliff of Moher. It was a hot, clear day with even here only a gentle breeze. Westward, left and right of where the picnickers sat, the cliff declining, exposed an open sea, quiet and luminous, yet hardly bluer than the blue sky. The land shelved downwards to the east in a composed, stripped pattern of green turf, grey walls and little houses painted white or pink or blue. There were no trees in sight. A few sheep grazed, and gulls and curlews cried, an empty road twisted between the fields like a slack white ribbon.

Angéle considered all this with wondering pleasure. Sharply outlined, clear, immaculate, and seeming on this day to overflow with light, the scene, dramatically balancing austerity with passion, surprised her very much and made her unwilling to cry out in hasty praise. Yet though so individual, so unlike other recollected scenes of beauty, it struck at her heart nostalgically, she felt: something it upheld of innocence, of positive goodness, familiarized it at this first encounter to emotional memory. It was austere and proud and extremely regional, yet it assaulted, even teased, imagination. Perhaps its beauty was in essence tragical; but it made Angéle feel very happy as she drank it in — made her laugh indeed.[1]

The technique used here is different from that in the previous passage. The scene is first described, as it were, objectively, and then through the sensibility of the girl observing it: her sensibility animates it. She sees it in terms of human feeling, balancing *austerity* with *passion*, suggesting *innocence* and *goodness*, perhaps even *tragedy*. This is ironic; for the people inhabiting the land of *The Last of Summer* prove unwelcoming to Angéle. They repudiate her: she is no more than a brief visitant.

So, either one leaves the alluring world or one is forced out. Seductive as it appears, the world offers no lasting place to man — all novelists tell us the same thing. Kate O'Brien's originality consists in using new material — the educated, middle-class of Ireland during the end of the last century and the beginning of this, and especially the girls and women of that class, as they struggle to escape from the lot of women everywhere — the condition of being the passive victims of the social mores of the time — as they endeavour to acquire an education which will enable them to earn their living, as they try to free themselves from the necessity of merely accepting love and, instead, attain to a position in which they can offer love. Kate O'Brien is never unaware of Christian Europe outside of Ireland, and how much Ireland has to learn from it. There was a common Europe of civilization and culture long before the Common Market of today. Kate O'Brien belonged to it: many of her heroines belong to it too. She detested the complacent self-regarding, Puritanic pietism of the thirties and forties in Ireland and saw it as an aberration from the great European tradition of Catholicism. St. Patrick, she reminds her readers in the journal, *Hibernia*, was a 'European gentleman'. Catholicism as a formative influence on character, as a shaping of the inner life, she valued; even when she had ceased to believe in Catholic doctrines. She exploited the dramatic possibilities it afforded, as any system which imposes on human creatures a rigorous abstract training to meet the inevitable assaults of the senses and the emotions must do. Tension and conflict necessarily result and tension and conflict are the stuff of drama.

Kate O'Brien shows her women possessing a moral life as much as men, indeed more than most men. They rely on their own knowledge, intelligence and instinct. In this she is heir to Jane Austen and Henry James, but she is also in another sense heir to the nineteenth-century Irish novelists, in whose work human feelings had been largely determined by historic factors, and human happiness is to be regarded as rendered impossible by economic pressures. It is the incompatibility between human expectations and the facts of existence, between human potentialities and the chances of their realization that mould the life of Kate O'Brien's characters, especially the life of her women characters. In short, she is a modern novelist.

After *As Music and Splendour* Kate O'Brien published no more novels, but she did not cease to write. In 1963, *Presentation Parlour* appeared, a memoir of her aunts, especially her mother's sisters, two of whom were nuns in the convent of the Presentation Order in Limerick, and in the parlour of which all the family gathered from time to time, as has already been recounted. She wrote an Irish travel book for Batsford, *My Ireland*, a highly selective and idiosyncratic account of her favourite places in Ireland. She contributed an occasional article to *The Irish Times*, written from her home in England and called *Long Distance*. She lectured to this body and that and she represented Ireland on the central committee of the *Comunita Europea degli Scrittori*, and in this capacity was often in Italy, and in 1962 visited Russia.

When in 1960 she returned to England, she had chosen to live in the village of Boughton, near Faversham, in Kent, not far from Canterbury, with its modern university, the University of Kent at Canterbury. She was in reach, therefore, of the society of academics, whose company she found at once congenial and irritating, as she always had done.

She enjoyed the village life of Boughton and was not far from London, which she could visit to meet friends or publishers as the need arose. I visited her in Boughton once, but the visit turned out a disaster. I developed a virus infection of the bronchial tract and gave it to my hostess! Everybody knows there is no worse sin a visitor can commit than this. I was supposed to be *en route* to France, but a shaken invalid crept home to Ireland as soon as she could, leaving an equally shaken invalid behind her. I mention the incident because it served to reveal the extraordinary kindness of Kate O'Brien's neighbours in Boughton: delicate soups and custards and jellies were brought to the bedsides of the stricken pair and a constant watch kept on their condition. If she had been living there all her life, she could not have received more attention.

I used to urge her at the time to write her autobiography — but in a sense this was stupid of me. She had already said what she wanted to say about her life in her novels, however obliquely. She was working on another novel during these years and she read me a couple of chapters before I fell a victim to that virus. It was set once again in Spain. I thought what I heard good and original, but she said she found it almost impossible to write nowadays: it had always been exquisitely difficult to say what one wanted to say but now it was almost insurmountably so. She no longer had the stamina that sustained attention to precision of meaning, to inventiveness of incident and the direction that narrative requires.

Kate O'Brien died on 13 August 1974 in the Kent and Canterbury Hospital. She used to say that one of the pleasures of living in Roundstone was the thought of being buried in the cemetery at Dog's Bay. But she also always said, 'Where the tree falls, let it lie.' So she was buried in Kent. Her favourite sister, Nance, was herself very ill and could not travel to attend the funeral. I was in Canada and did not know until all was over.

Kate O'Brien's work is now part of Irish literature and is taking on for young people an historical dimension. They see her as revealing a side of Irish life and aspects of Irish character that otherwise would be unknown to them. She would have been pleased with this. But, of course, such an assessment could never have been made while she was alive. One has to be dead to become part of history: only dead, can the writer, ironically, be known.

NOTES

I   ORIGINS AND EARLY LIFE
1   *My Ireland*. (B. T. Batsford, London, 1962) p. 23.
2   P. S. O'Hegarty, *The History of Ireland since the Union* (Methuen, London, 1952) p. 463.
3   T. Crofton Croker, *Researches in the South of Ireland*, 1824, reprinted Irish University Press, pp. 226-227.
4   *University Review*, Vol. III, No. 2, p. 7
5   *Pray for the Wanderer* (Penguin Books, Harmondsworth, 1951) p. 142.
6   *University Review*, Vol. III, No. 4. p. II.

II   THE FAMILY: *WITHOUT MY CLOAK*
1   John Galsworthy. *The Man of Property*, (First published 1906, reprinted Penguin Books, Harmondsworth 1951), p. II.
2   *Without My Cloak* (William Heinemann, London, 1931) p. 280.
3   *Ibid.*, p. 462.

IV   A GIRL AND HER BEAUTY: *MARY LAVELLE*
1   *Mary Lavelle* (Heinemann Pocket Edition, London 1947) p. 185.
2   *Ibid.*, p. 226.

V   THE NUN: *THE LAND OF SPICES*
1   *The Land of Spices* (Arlen House Reprint, Dublin, 1982), pp. 117-118.

VI   THE GREAT LADY: *THAT LADY*
1   *University Review*, Vol. III, No. 4. pp. 7-8.

VII   ASIDES: *PRAY FOR THE WANDERER* and *THE LAST OF SUMMER*
1   *Pray for the Wanderer* (Penguin Books, Harmondsworth 1951) p.47.
2   *Ibid.*, pp. 107-108.
3   *Ibid.*, p. 111.

X   FOREIGN SETTINGS
Part of this chapter was read as a paper at the 1984 IASAIL Conference at Graz.
1   *Mary Lavelle, Ed. cit*, p. 17.
2   *Ibid.*, pp. 51-52.
3   *Ibid.*, pp. 88-89.
4   *Ibid.*, p. 227.

XIV   CONCLUSION
1   *The Last of Summer* (Arlen House Reprint, Dublin 1982), p. 62.

INDEX